Chinese Tea Culture

by Wang Ling

FOREIGN LANGUAGES PRESS

First Edition   2000
Second Printing   2002

Home Page:
http://www.flp.com.cn
E-mail Addresses:
Info@flp.com.cn
Sales@flp.com.cn

ISBN 7-119-02144-3

© Foreign Languages Press, Beijing, China, 2000

Published by Foreign Languages Press
24 Baiwanzhuang Road, Beijing 100037, China
Distributed by China International Book Trading Corporation
35 Chegongzhuang Xilu, Beijing 100044, China
P.O. Box 399, Beijing, China

Printed in the People's Republic of China

Contents

Preface

China, the Hometown of Tea Culture

The tea tree, a perennial evergreen bush, belongs to the camellia family. The processed tea plays an important role in people's social life. A common Chinese saying runs, "When we get up in the morning, the first things we should get ready are firewood, rice, edible oil, salt, soy, vinegar and tea," which demonstrates tea is a necessity of life. Whenever we sit round a table, or have a get-together with good friends, a cup of fragrant tea will give a rich flavor to the occasion. In ancient times, many emperors were addicted to tea. Once, during the Qing Dynasty, Emperor Kangxi (on the throne from 1662 to 1722) arrived at Taihu Lake in Suzhou on his third inspection tour of the south of the Yangtze River, when someone offered him a cup of tea named "frightening and killing tea." After drinking it, Kangxi thought that the tea tasted really nice but that its name was not very elegant. So, knowing that it was picked on the Biluo Peak in spring, he named it Biluochun and added it to the list of recognized tribute items. His grandson, Emperor Qianglong (on the throne from 1736 to 1795), also liked tea very much. In the first lunar month of each year, he would hold a tea party on an auspicious day, drinking tea and composing poems.

It is universally acknowledged that China is the original tea-growing area, as well as the first country to grow, produce and drink tea. Then, when did China find and start to use tea? According to the *Holy Farmer's Herbal Classic*, 2,700 years ago, the Holy Farmer tasted various herbs he picked, and often got poisoned. Later, he found a plant, tea, which could detoxify him. This story shows that people in ancient times treated tea only as a medicinal herb. It took quite a long time for tea to be used as a drink rather than a herb. Wang Bao mentioned in his "A Contract with a Child Servant," which was written in 59 B.C, that the child servant should boil tea for his master and go to Wuyang (east of Pengxian County, Sichuan Province, then a famous tea market) to buy tea. This evidence reveals that tea, as a drink, started not later than the Western Han Period. In the Three Kingdoms Period (220-280), King of the Dongwu State Sun Hao (242-283) ordered his ministers to drink liquor and gained pleasure from their drunkenness each time he entertained them. Minister Wei Yao could not drink, so Sun Hao gave him tea secretly and let him drink tea instead of liquor. From then on, treating guests to tea became gradually popular among scholars.

In the Northern and Southern Dynasties (420-589), Buddhism became popular and monks refreshed themselves with tea when sitting in meditation and chanting scriptures. Drinking tea became widespread in big and small temples, where tea trees were grown and tea drinking was studied. This was called the integration of tea and Buddhism.

In the Tang Dynasty (618-907), tea drinking achieved even greater popularity. Since tea could stimulate their thinking, scholars took delight in it and wrote poems and painted pictures using it as the theme. At that time, tea trees grew in Sichuan, Hunan, Hubei, Jiangxi and Fujian provinces and many other places, and the trade volume of tea rapidly increased. Tang poet Bai Juyi wrote, "The businessman stressed profits and belittled the affection for his wife. The month before last he went to Fuliang to buy tea." Fuliang (today's Jingdezhen, Jiangxi Province) was then a distribution center of tea. The businessman gained profit by transporting tea for sale and often rashly took leave of his wife for business. During this period, Lu Yu (733-804) summed up his predecessors' experience of tea and wrote *The Book of Tea*, the first book about tea in the world. In the book, he systematically related the origin of tea, its nature, history and growing area, as well as describing tools for picking tea, processes of producing tea, methods of drinking tea and drinking vessels. Later, he was called the "Saint of Tea."

In the Song (960-1279) and Yuan (1271-1368) dynasties a popular custom was tea appraising. To win the appraisal, the tea owner had to have top-quality tea, which was the most important factor, high-quality water, and teasets of exquisite appearance and nice colors to fully set off the color of the tea. Over the long history of drinking tea, a special and simple Chinese tea culture came into being. Drinking tea was not only for quenching thirst or for enjoyment, but also for the promotion of friendship and mutual understanding. In addition, tea inspired many kinds of cultural activity. For example, the tea-related poems and paintings left by scholars, as well as the songs, dances and local operas about tea, show the close relationship between tea and spiritual experience. Folk customs of drinking tea reflected the ancient Chinese people's great interest in tea culture. The most typical example was the teahouses dotting the streets and lanes of Chinese towns. People from high officials and noble lords to commoners liked to gather at teahouses. Businessmen exchanged information about business, fellow-villagers gathered to extend greetings, and scholars exchanged ideas while drinking tea there. Even disputes among the people were judged and mediated in the teahouses. At teahouses, people could also enjoy variety shows and storytelling. It can truly be said that teahouses were a microcosm of the social life of China as well as its political, economic and cultural center. Today, the famous teahouses in China include the Lao She Teahouse in Beijing, the Taotaoju Teahouse in Guangzhou, and the Bayu Teahouse in Chongqing. In Guangzhou, people go to teahouses every day enjoying two cups of tea and light refreshments. In Sichuan, people can sit or lie on a row of bamboo chairs, drinking tea while talking about everything under the sun. The teahouses in Beijing have a more cultural flavor, which encompassed drinking tea and eating snacks, enjoying folk art forms, making friends and doing research.

People often used tea as a betrothal gift, for it could not be "transplanted." After accepting tea as a betrothal gift, a girl could not capriciously change her decision to marry her fiance. According to *A Dream of Red Mansions*, written by Cao Xueqin in the Qing Dynasty, Wang Xifeng said to Lin Daiyu, "Since you have drunk our tea, why not be our sister-in-law?" This literary quotation is an example of "accepting tea."

Entertainment of guests to tea is the most fundamental social behavior in the Chinese people's contacts with each other. When a guest comes, the Chinese will offer him or her a cup of tea to express friendship. A poem says, "When a guest came to my home from afar at a cold night, I hastily lit bamboo firewood to make tea to treat him."

China is the home country of tea. Before the Tang Dynasty, Chinese tea was exported by land and sea, first to Japan and Korea, then to India and Central Asia and, in the Ming and Qing dynasties, to the Arabian Peninsula. In the early period of the 17th century, Chinese tea was exported to Europe, where the upper class adopted the fashion of drinking tea. Chinese tea, like Chinese silk and china, made an outstanding contribution to the world's material and spiritual civilization.

With Chinese tea and tea culture as the object of study, this book deals with the origin of tea, its history, the methods and customs of drinking tea, drinking vessels and other rich and vivid information. In this book the reader can read many interesting stories about Chinese tea and tea culture.

Xiao Yi Wrangles Over the Masterpiece of Calligraphy Lan Ting, by Yan Liben of the Tang Dynasty

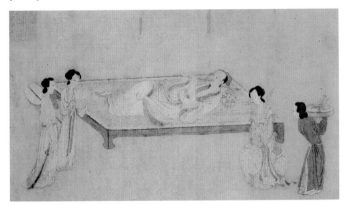

Auspiciousness and Happiness, by Zhang Xuan of the Tang Dynasty

Han Xizai Attending an Evening Banquet, by Gu Hongzhong of the Five Dynasties

Children Playing in Spring, by Su Hanchen of the Song Dynasty

Compatriots with One Mind, painted in the Yuan Dynasty

Enjoying the Moon, by Leng Mei of the Qing Dynasty

Teahouse, painted in the early Republic of China period

Yangliuqing woodcut of the Qing Dynasty

Tea bowls and pots of the Tang Dynasty

Teapots of the Ming Dynasty

Teapots of the Qing Dynasty

Teapots of the Qing Dynasty

Chapter 1
The Origin of Tea Drinking and the Embryo of Tea Culture

The Holy Farmer Tasting Herbs

This book tells of the spirit and culture of tea. But, our study begins with the material effect and the use of tea as a drink.

The discovery and the use of tea in China can be traced back to the ancient time of Holy Farmer (a legendary ruler, the second of the Three August Ones, who was supposed to have invented the plough and discovered the curative virtues of plants). The Chinese people often call themselves descendants of Yan Di and the Yellow Emperor. According to historians' research of the texts, Yan Di refers to the Holy Farmer. About 5,000 years ago, the Holy Farmer, who was thought of as the God of Farming, invented many farm tools and taught people how to grow crops. China is a country where the ancient farming revolution was accomplished very early. Archaeological excavation and historical records prove it is a reliable fact rather than a legend that the Holy Farmer founded methods of agricultural production. The Holy Farmer was also the God of Medicine in Chinese legend. To save the common people from pain, the Holy Farmer selected various wild plants as medicine. Fearless of the sacrifice, he tasted the wild plants himself to learn their effect on the human body. It is said that one day he got poisoned seventy-two times when gathering and tasting herbs on a mountain. Later he found a plant, which was tea. He brewed the leaves in a pottery tripod and then drank the liquid. As a result, the toxins in his body disappeared. Since then, the Chinese people have treated tea as a precious medicine bestowed on human beings by the cosmos. The story illustrates that the Chinese people first used tea as medicine.

Early in the Zhou Dynasty (c. the 11th century-771 B.C.), tea was used as medicine by people from commoners to the royal family. For example, the Sichuan people paid tribute, including tea, to the Wu Emperor (living in about the 11th century B.C.) of the Zhou Dynasty. In the *Ritual of Zhou* (an ancient Chinese codex and record reportedly written by Lord Zhou about 3,000 years ago) there are more records about the officials in charge of the use of tea in the royal court of the Zhou Dynasty.

Some people think that tea was regarded simply as a vegetable for some time. However, tea was specially used as a magical drink in the Han Dynasty (206 B.C.-A.D. 220). In the Han Dynasty tea was universally grown, laying a foundation for its wide use. In the famous Tombs of the Han Dynasty (built in the second century B.C.) at Mawangdui, Changsha, Hunan Province, a box of tea was discovered. In tombs of the reign of Wendi (on the throne from 179 B.C. to 156 B.C.) in Jiangling, Hubei Province, a corpse and a box of tea were found. All these finds show that in the early Han Dynasty nobles used tea and buried it with the dead as a treasure.

After discovering tea, the Chinese people used it as a medicinal herb, a vegetable, and a drink successively over 3,000 years. During this period, the use of tea did not have a spiritual dimension, though it was used as a magical medicinal herb. The great leap for tea occurred once it began to be used as a drink instead of a medicinal herb.

2

Scholars of the Han Dynasty and Tea

Generally speaking, the use of something and the formation of a custom begins with the common people. But it is of interest to note that tea's being used as a drink started among a group of high-level scholars.

Tea drinking was formally recorded in Chinese documents. "A Contract with a Child Servant," which was written by Wang Bao in the year 59 B.C. in the Han Dynasty, tells an interesting story. In the Western Han Dynasty, there was a man named Wang Ziyuan from Sichuan who went to Chengdu to take an exam. He put up at the house of his late friend, where his friend's widow, Yang Hui, still lived. Perhaps Yang Hui adored Wang Ziyuan for she received him warmly, and let her child servant, Bian Liao, serve the guest with considerate actions, such as buying and brewing tea. Unhappy with this, Bian Liao ran to his late master's tomb, complaining tearfully. "My good Master, you bought me and let me look after your house as a child servant, but you did not let me serve your wife's lover!" Learning about this, Yang Hui and Wang Ziyuan became very angry. They decided that Wang Ziyuan would spend 15,000 coins to change Bian Liao's status to that of a servant of Wang Ziyuan so that Bian Liao dared not revolt. Wang Ziyuan drew up a contract to buy a servant titled "A Contract with a Child Servant," which stipulated what Bian Liao should do every day, including buying tea at Wuyang Market and brewing tea carefully and then carefully cleaning and putting away the teasets. The details of the contract show that at the time scholars were very particular about drinking tea.

Besides Wang Ziyuan, many famous writers in the Han Dynasty took a liking to tea. The prose-poetry, which was popular at the time, was an ancient style with its own aesthetic ideas and meters. Sima Xiangru and Yang Xiong, two famous experts in

舍中有客，提壺行酤，汲水作餔〈滌杯整桉，音鵰〉，魚炰鼈，烹茶〈煮茶以苦為菜，茄也〉盡具備已蓋藏，關門塞竇，餵豬縱犬，勿與鄰里爭鬥。奴但當飯豆飲水，不得嗜酒，欲飲美酒，唯得染唇漬口，不得傾盂覆斗，不得辰出夜入，交關伴偶。舍後有樹，當裁作船，上至江州〈漢中郡有江州縣，蜀都賦府用椽錢庸之，吏直〉，下到煎主，為府椽求用錢，推紡惡敗〈郎官山洛水〉，傻索綿亭〈其綿亭地名，席出地名〉買席，往來都洛〈枲切麻也，禹貢，地志地理，廣理直〉。當為婦女求脂澤，販於小市〈桌切麻也販出，小路〉，牽犬〈武陽桌頁販也，出小禹貢，悉〉。

蜀郡〈放也，字樞索之，所以治串錢注有章工官水〉所出布新都〈新都各入縣，有〉，主樞索之所，放也。販放一市，作鵝武陽買茶，楊氏池中擔荷〈卜膏沐，鈇鈌，歸都擔枲轉出旁蹉，武陽地名，其名茶茗，其花芙氏，大〉。

prose-poetry, liked drinking tea very much. When still unknown to the public, Sima Xiangru was involved in a charming love story. According to the Chinese feudal code of ethics of the time, one's marriage, especially a girl's marriage, should be decided by his or her parents. But Sima Xiangru met a girl with different ideas named Zhuo Wenjun, who bravely ran away with him. Being badly off, they ran a shop selling food. Their experience is told in the well-known story Wenjun in Charge of Her Shop. The story gives no account of whether he sold liquor or tea, but Sima Xiangru wrote about tea and even if he did not sell tea, he at least showed interest in drinking it. The second famous expert, Yang Xiong, wrote about tea in his *Dialect*. Of course, famous men of letters like Sima Xiangru often entered the royal court, where drinking tea had become a fashion. An ancient Chinese novel relates an interesting tale about drinking tea in the royal court. After the Cheng Emperor of the Han Dynasty died, his concubine Zhao Feiyan met him in a dream. As she presented tea to him, the Emperor's attendants said that he must not drink it as she had failed to wait upon him respectfully and carefully. Zhao Feiyan cried out in her dream and then awoke. The story shows that early in the Han Dynasty serving tea was regarded in the royal court as a serious matter of etiquette and that badly behaved people were disqualified from serving tea.

Zhu Geliang, Prime Minister of the State of Shu during the Three Kingdoms Period (A.D. 220-A.D. 280), is known to almost every household. His wisdom and civil and military abilities are still respected by later generations. Tradition says that Zhu Geliang popularized tea cultivation in Yunnan Province and other places. Since Zhu Geliang was also called Kongming, people from Yunnan Province to this day call the ancient tea shrub "Kongming Tree."

In the Jin Dynasty (A.D. 220-A.D. 280) poet Zhang Zai wrote in his "A Poem at Chengdu Tower," "On drinking tea, I think of the elegant living rooms of the experts at prose-poetry Yang Xiong and Sima Xiangru, and their forceful and beautiful proses and verses."

Why was drinking tea initially stressed by great scholars? Perhaps it was because they drew their inspiration from drinking tea or that tea reminded them of beautiful mountains and waters or that it calmed them and helped them in their philosophic thinking about the cosmos. Whatever the reason, as soon as tea was used as a drink, it blended with the spirit of scholars as if it itself had had sagacity. According to Buddhism, all things on earth have sagacity, and man can communicate with nature. So perhaps tea is the most sagacious representative of plants.

The Extravagance of the Eastern and Western Jin Dynasties and the Northern and Southern Dynasties and the Cultivation of Incorruptibility with Tea

In the Han Dynasty, Chinese rulers advocated thrift. In the early Western Han Dynasty, the Emperor rode in ox carts and did not take carriages readily. In the Eastern Han Dynasty (A.D. 25- A.D. 220), the country became rich but cultural intercourse and the code of ethics still advocated filial piety, friendship, honesty and uprightness. Even some officials were incorruptible and thrifty. Official Xuan Bing distributed fields among the poor, and offered his clans his own salary although he stored no rice in his home. Official Wang Liang did not let his wife live in his official residence. Even if there were few such officials in the feudal society, they reflect the simple and friendly virtues of the Chinese people from time immemorial.

However, in the Eastern and Western Jin dynasties (A.D. 265-A.D. 420) and the Northern and Southern dynasties (A.D.

420-A.D. 589), the social mood changed greatly. Nobles competed with each other in extravagance. In the Jin Dynasty Official He Zeng went even further than the Emperor, being extravagant in clothes, chariots and food. He spent 10,000 coins on food every day while his son spent 20,000 coins. Not to be outdone, Ren Kai, a rich man, spent 20,000 coins every meal. Shi Chong, known as "money bag," had rare delicacies from land and water at each meal, and used brocade as his barricade and wax as his firewood. He even wore a new suit each time after he went out of the lavatory, beside which more than ten maidservants stood. In the Southern Dynasty, Emperor Liangwu (A.D. 502-550) was thrifty while his brother, Xiao Hong, lived in luxury. He was reported to have built many private storehouses. Emperor Liangwu went there to investigate fearing that this brother of his was hiding weapons for rebellion. He found that in the storehouses were piles of treasures and silk instead of weapons. As well, there were thirty houses specially for storing more than 300 million coins.

All these excesses worried sober-minded rulers who advocated cultivation of incorruptibility to change the luxurious ways. In this attempt, tea played a role.

Compared to a man, tea is by nature clean and pure. It absorbs rain and dew in high mountains, and grows green leaves. It blossoms gorgeously in the glow of morning and evening, and takes root in the bosom of mountains. In ancient China, people thought that tea should never be transplanted and because of this they praised tea for its great tenacity. Perhaps due to these virtues of tea, they countered luxury with tea.

The Eastern Jin Dynasty official Lu Na was incorruptible. As a prefecture chief he would not accept a salary. Later the imperial court recalled him and appointed him to the position of Left Service Official. When his family asked him how many boats of things were to be loaded, he only wanted the grains needed on the journey.

The rest were to be sealed and made a public possession. When Lu Na acted as prefecture chief of Wuxing, a well-known senior general, Xie An, planned to visit him. Lu Na's nephew thought that such a noble guest should be treated with consideration. When he saw that his uncle had not made any preparations, he decided to act on his own. After Xie An arrived, Lu Na treated him to only tea and fruit. Seeing this, Xie's nephew gave a grand banquet for fear of neglecting the guest. After the guest left, Lu Na said resentfully, "You did not win honor for me, but just smeared my clean virtue." The opinionated nephew received a good beating. Afterwards this tale became a favorite, with many people following its example. Huan Wen, a man of Lu Na's time, also advocated drinking tea instead of liquor. Statesman though he was, Huan Wen had considerable military ability. Having won many battles, he enjoyed a good reputation. In terms of advocating the cultivation of incorruptibility, he thought highly of Lu Na. When he asked Lu Na his capacity for liquor, Lu Na said he could drink only two cups. Huan Wen said, "I can drink only three cups with ten slices of meat. At banquets I usually treat guests to some tea and seven plates of fruit."

In the Southern and Northern dynasties, some emperors drank tea instead of liquor to show their simplicity. In the Southern Qi Dynasty Emperor Shizu was enlightened. During the ten years of his reign there were almost no general battles, and the common people were able to recuperate and multiply. He disliked amusement as it could waste too much property. When he knew that he was dying, he issued a testamentary edict that his funeral should not be held sumptuously and the common people should not be troubled too much. He said that in his memorial ceremony only several plates of cooked rice and fruit and a cup of tea rather than the traditional "three sacrifices" would be offered. In addition, he required that from then on anyone, noble or lowly, should obey the same rule. Of course, it is hard to say whether later emperors and officials obeyed the rule; but at the time his will set a good example to nobles in the curbing of extravagance. From around that time, tea began to be offered as a sacrifice in China.

Ancient Metaphysicians and Tea Drinking

In the later period of the Eastern Jin Dynasty, China was disrupted and the Southern and Northern dynasties emerged. The north was in chaos caused by war, while the south was richly endowed and seldom touched by war. So scholars often gathered and held "cultural salons," discussing literature, philosophy and other issues. They were called "talkers." Most early talkers liked to drink liquor. They often drank liquor as they discussed matters beside clean waters and green hills. Among them were the famous "seven worthies in the bamboo forest." One talker called Liu Ling gave his name to a liquor that was reportedly his favorite. This famous "Liu Ling Liquor" is well-known in China even today. But later, the talkers began to drink tea instead of liquor for two reasons: Liquor could drive people mad and affect their discussion, and the poor scholars could not afford to buy liquor, which was costly and had to be drunk with meat. Therefore, most talkers of the later period drank tea. For example, the famous talker Wang Meng liked drinking tea very much. When scholars had free discussions in his home, they were certainly plied with tea. A few people who did not like tea much humorously called the talks in Wang Meng's home "water disasters."

If the "cultivation of incorruptibility with tea" advocated by Lu Na, Huan Wen and others symbolized the spirit of tea, the talkers' habit of drinking tea to keep sober and to inspire their thinking reflected the direct effect of tea on people's spiritual sphere.

9

During the Southern and Northern dynasties, which was a period of cultural exchange, the trend of thought called metaphysics arose. The metaphysicians researched Taoism, which was blended with Confucianism. Most were distinguished. They stressed family status, composure and manners, liked free fantasy, and analyzed profound theories about nature and society in relation to all things on earth. They liked to give lectures with hundreds, even thousands, of listeners at times. Such all-day lectures surely made them feel dry. Unlike people at parties, who can have their own way, lecturers must talk and behave properly, and think clearly. So tea was indispensable to lectures. Since tea made people excited yet sober and quenched their thirst, talkers praised it highly. For metaphysicians, the material and spiritual effects of tea were perfectly unified. Thus, from the start, tea culture was coated with the mysterious flavor of eastern philosophy.

Immortals and Tea Drinking

The oldest cultural principle in China is Taoism, which has a much longer history than Confucianism. Taoists hold that man is an integral part of nature, and stress that man is in harmony with the universe and nature. In the Han Dynasty, Taoist thoughts developed into Taoism. Taoism advocated overcoming the common people's mortal failings and tapping special intellectual resources through the training of one's body and soul. The Chinese people call those who succeed in practicing asceticism immortals, and think that they have special wisdom and miraculous powers like God. Later, Indian Buddhism spread to China. Since the Chinese people did not fully understand this early Buddhism, they took it for granted that Buddhist and Taoist immortals were alike when they saw

Buddhists sat in meditation like Taoists. They regarded all Taoists and Buddhists as immortals. During the Southern and Northern dynasties, Confucians, Taoists and Buddhists debated their beliefs. It is interesting to note that no matter how much their ideas were opposed, none excluded tea and they all liked to make friends over tea. In literary works and fairy tales of the time there were many stories about immortals and tea. According to Chinese ancient books and records, during the reign of Yuan Di Emperor in the Jin Dynasty, there was an old lady, who often sold tea at the market. Though the tea was poured into cups from morning till night, her kettle was full all the time. The old lady helped the poor with income from her tea sales, but local authorities were displeased with her and put her into prison. But at night the merciful old lady flew away with her teasets from the window of the prison. Chinese ancients held that immortals could fly, so the old lady was of course thought of as an immortal. Other Chinese documents relate that in the Southern Dynasty a monk Fa Yao, who liked to drink tea, died at the age of ninety-nine. His vast age was due to the magical properties of tea. A man of such advanced years was treated as an immortal, since in ancient times living conditions were harsh and there was no modern scientific medical treatment. Also, according to documents, Dan Qiuzi and Huang Shanjun recast themselves and lived as famous immortals due to drinking tea.

Why did the Chinese people connect tea with immortals? Because, according to the Taoists' theory of keeping good health, man's vitality lies in collateral channels, which tea helps to dredge. In addition, tea, which could keep people sober-minded and quiet, was deemed a necessity to practice Taoism or Buddhism as both advocated sitting in meditation. Thus, the effect of tea drinking was connected with the oldest oriental philosophy, rules of keeping good health, and an elevation in the spiritual sphere.

Summary

From the above, we can see that tea has survived more than three thousand years since it was discovered and used, first as a medicinal herb and then as a common drink.

From the Han Dynasty, tea has been planted and formally used as a drink. Owing to its special functions and its spiritual effect, from the beginning it was stressed by scholars and thinkers. Writers, talkers, metaphysicians, statesmen, and people in religious circles took a liking to drinking it. Its sweet scent, mildness and fragrance attracted people.

However, the spiritual and cultural effects of tea were not catalogued at that time. Ways of drinking tea had not become an art form as they were to later; nor did they form a philosophy that enlightened people's thought and emotion. Tea culture was embryonic from the time of the Han Dynasty, when tea drinking formally appeared in records, to the Southern and Northern dynasties, when tea was used by philosophers and immortals. It was in the Tang Dynasty that the real Chinese tea culture, including tea art, the tea ceremony and a complete expression of cultural philosophy, came into being.

Chapter 2
The Sprouting and Blooming of China's Tea Culture

China's Tea Culture Sprouted in the Tang Dynasty

Tang People's Love for Tea

China's tea culture took its initial shape in the Tang Dynasty (618-907), the heyday of China's feudal age. The economic, social and cultural prosperity and busy foreign exchanges at that time provided rich soil for the sprouting of the splendid tea culture of Tang.

During the period the tea plant was cultivated in 42 prefectures of the country, and the habit of drinking tea had filtered into the daily life of people of all social ranks and classes. Emperors of the later Tang, who were especially fond of tea, ordered the tea-producing areas to send their earliest tea, which was also the best, to the palace, where a grand banquet was held on 5 April every year to celebrate the Qingming Festival, the Han festival to honor the dead, which is also called Plant Festival. Some officials even got promoted because they paid the tea tribute. A satirical ballad ran: "The father wins promotion through tea, which also brings the son riches; hence why don't the intellectuals go a short cut like this instead of troubling so much to study the *Spring and Autumn* and *A*

Horseback Diagram from the Yellow River?" To win the emperor's love, imperial concubines racked their brains to improve the art of making tea, and gradually a game called tea competition was developed among them. In the Tang Dynasty intellectuals aiming to secure official positions had to go through strict examinations, the final of which was held in the capital and directly presided over by the emperor. In the exam, supervised by many court officials, candidates were shut in separate rooms to avoid cheating and only allowed to take some solid food with them. The only exception was tea which could be sent to each room for the examinee to refresh himself. Princes and ministers, following the example of the emperor, took pride in their good taste for tea. Li Deyu, the grand councilor, even took the trouble to use the best spring water from thousands of miles away to make a cup of tea. It was customary to receive guests with tea and regarded as most impolite not to do so.

Drinking tea was initially advocated by intellectuals, and the habit as well as the art of poetry prospered during the Tang Dynasty. Liquor had always been used by poets to encourage themselves to write, but in the Tang Dynasty alcohol was officially prohibited and production greatly reduced, because it needed too much grain. So tea, a much cheaper stimulant, was used as an alternative. At the time Buddhism was flourishing, and monks in temples were required to sit in meditation in the evening without supper. But young monks always found it difficult. So the Lingyan Temple at Mount Tai made an exception, allowing the monks to have tea during the evening practice. It was not long before the measure spread across the temples of the whole country and became common. Gradually tea also became a sacrifice to the Buddha and a special beverage for distinguished visitors. Because of the large consumption of tea, temples began to grow tea plants themselves. Because they were mostly located in mountains with plentiful rainfall and sunshine, temples always produced tea of good quality.

It was also no coincidence that Taoists, who also lived in seclusion in mountains, had a green thumb as well as a good taste for tea.

With the popularity of drinking tea among ordinary people, tea shops appeared everywhere, even in the Central Plains provinces, such as Shandong, Hunan and Shanxi, where tea production was comparatively low.

The tea trade, a useful means for the Tang Dynasty to increase state revenue, was also employed to promote exchanges with neighboring ethnic groups. Bartering tea for horses was very common in border areas at the time.

The Tang people's universal love for tea gave impetus to research into tea. Ten main functions of tea were summarized as follows:

1. Tea is beneficial to health and able to dredge body channels and relieve headaches, xerophthalmia and fatigue;

2. Tea can help dispel the effects of alcohol and quit drinking;

3. Tea, when dressed with sauces, can serve as nourishing "porridge" to allay hunger;

4. Tea can help drive away summer heat;

5. Tea, a good refresher, can help shake off drowsiness;

6. Tea can help people to purify themselves and eliminate worries;

7. Tea can help the digestion of greasy food, making it indispensable in the life of Chinese ethnic minority people, whose staple foods are meat and milk products;

8. Tea can be used to eliminate toxins from the body;

9. Tea is conducive to longevity;

10. Tea can aid self knowledge.

Lu Yu, the Saint of Tea

Chinese people always attach the same importance to the

quality of their material and their spiritual lives. For instance, they eat and drink to satisfy their physiological requirements, and to refresh and form their minds as well. Drinking alcohol, always regarded as etiquette at banquets and sacrificial ceremonies, is also customary for soldiers who are to go into battle to show their heroism and boldness. Chinese people are particular about the aroma, color and taste of their food dishes, which are taken not only to fill the stomach, but also as objects with aesthetic value.

So naturally, tea, a drink specially advocated by intellectuals, became a material full of cultural and ideological meaning. It was the Tang people who further developed the art of making and drinking tea, imbuing the whole process with the rhyme of a poem and making the drinker meditate on the philosophy of life. Lu Yu, the first person who perfected the art of tea, created the tea ceremony and promoted tea culture, was addressed respectfully as the "Saint of Tea" in Chinese history.

Lu Yu, born at Jingling, Fuzhou (present-day Tianmen County in Hubei Province), lived during Tang's flourishing ages of Kaiyuan and Tianbao. An orphan abandoned by his parents, he was taken in by Jigong, an elderly eminent Buddhist, and brought up in a temple named Longgai. Jigong loved tea very much and grew many tea plants around the temple. Little Lu Yu learned many arts of cultivating and making tea from Jigong, and gradually became an expert. According to legend, once when Jigong was called up to teach Buddhism at the imperial court, he felt quite disappointed at the tea there. But one day he was suddenly overjoyed after taking several sips of tea, saying, "Ah, it's made by my disciple Lu Yu. He's come." It was true. Lu Yu had been specially summoned to make tea for him.

Though growing up in a Buddhist temple, Lu Yu was more interested in Confucianism. The reclusive life in a lonely temple was too much for him. So he managed to flee away and join a theatrical troupe. As he was clever, he not only acted but also wrote many humorous plays. Later he won the recognition of Li Qiwu, prefect of Jingling, who helped him to go to nearby Mount Tianmen to learn Confucianism from an old scholar. But the good times did not last long. Lu Yu's study was interrupted by An Lushan's Revolt in the north, which drove the emperor Tang Xuanzong south to Sichuan from the capital Chang'an. Lu Yu was forced to go with the fugitives to Huzhou, a tea-growing area in the south. There he collected much useful information about the cultivation, picking and baking of tea, and also made friends with the most famous poets, monks, calligraphers and statesmen of the period through their mutual love of tea. On the basis of profound discussion with his friends on the art of making and drinking tea and his own long-term exploration of the theory of tea culture, Lu Yu wrote *The Book of Tea*, the first treatise on tea and tea culture in the world.

The Book of Tea by Lu Yu and the Tea Culture in the Tang Dynasty

The *Book of Tea* contains ten chapters. The first chapter deals with the origin of tea, the soil and climate suitable for its cultivation and its nature and functions. Chapters two and three cover the equipment for the processing of tea and the actual processing. Chapter Four looks at utensils for making and drinking tea; Chapter Five deals with making tea and the arts applicable to tea-making; Chapter Six explores the technique of drinking tea and standards of tea appreciation. Chapter Seven records the history of Chinese people's tea-drinking habits while Chapter Eight describes China's tea-producing areas and the qualities of different teas. Chapter Nine outlines the numbers of tea-related things to be used on different occasions and the final chapter details tea paintings and advocates using this vivid art form to introduce tea to tea drinkers.

一之源
二之具
三之造

竟陵陸　羽　撰

一之源

茶者南方之嘉木也一尺二尺迺至數十尺其巴山峽川有兩人合抱者伐而掇之其樹如瓜蘆葉如梔子花如白薔薇實如栟櫚葉如丁香根如胡桃（瓜蘆木出廣州似茶至苦澀栟櫚蒲葵之屬其子似茶胡桃與茶根皆下孕兆至瓦礫苗木上抽）

其字或從草或從木或草木并（從草當作茶其字出開元文字音義從木當作搽其字出）

其名一曰茶二曰檟三曰蔎四曰茗五曰荈（周公云檟苦茶楊執戟云蜀西南人謂茶曰蔎郭弘農云早取為茶晚取為茗或一曰荈耳）

其地上者生爛石中者生櫟壤下者生黃土凡藝

The *Book of Tea* is not only a treatise on tea, but also a reflective synthesis of natural and social sciences and the material and ideological world. It creates an art of the process of drinking tea, including its baking, water selection, the display of teasets and drinking, all of which are imbued with an aesthetic atmosphere. The book also accentuates the moral factor in the art of tea. Lu Yu held that people who loved drinking tea should excel in virtue. He made the golden mean of Confucianists, the perseverence of Buddhists in seeking truth and the Taoists' theory that man is an integral part of nature all blend harmoniously in the process of drinking tea, allowing the drinker to attain mental purity in the aroma of tea. The *Book of Tea* is regarded as the authoritative summary of Chinese tea culture before the mid-Tang period. Later Tang thinkers continued to write works on tea culture, such as the *Sixteen Varieties of Tea* by Su Yi, which added new ideas to the art of tea, and the *Comments on the Waters for Making Tea* by Zhang Youxin, which detailed the value of the water in the rivers, springs, pools and lakes of the whole country. Liu Zhenliang, a eunuch who had reached a high level of attainment in tea culture, even summarized the ten virtues of tea. However, these thinkers were only experts standing on the shoulders of Lu Yu, who pioneered tea culture and became the saint of tea in the eye of later generations. Late in the Tang Dynasty Lu Yu was posthumously called the God of Tea. In China gods did not come from Heaven, but were seen as the spirits of great people. Lu Yu, an eminent contributor to the culture of tea, was undoubtedly worthy of the title.

Tribute Tea and Game Tea in the Song Dynasty

In the Tang Dynasty the habit of drinking tea spread from the imperial court to towns and the countryside; and it was the literati, hermits and Buddhists who played a leading role in the advocacy of tea culture. But things changed in the Song Dynasty (960-1279), when the influence of intellectuals on the culture of tea weakened. Although many famous literati, such as Su Shi, the great writer of the Northern Song, and Li Qingzhao, the celebrated woman poet, and Lu You, a prolific poet of the Southern Song, were fond of tea and wrote some literary pieces on tea, they contributed little to the construction of tea culture. Tea culture at that time was expanded and publicized by two polar strengths—the imperial court and ordinary people.

Tribute Tea in the Song Dynasty

Song emperors had a special love of tea, and some of them were well up in the tea ceremony. Emperor Song Huizong even wrote a treatise on tea, entitled *Grand View on Tea*. Because of the supreme standing of the emperor, the natural and artistic qualities of the tea given as tribute to the imperial court were seriously taken by tea makers.

It had been a tradition down the ages to compress tea leaves into cakes for storage. When the tea culture was in bloom, the Song people, in order to add to the beauty of tea, began to make such cakes in a more ingenious way and have the imperial dragon or phoenix pattern embossed on them. Such tribute tea was mainly produced in the Jianzhou Prefecture, and designed by two famous officials, Ding Wei and Cai Xiang.

Jianzhou, a prefecture originally called Jian'an, was located in present-day Fujian Province. A place with beautiful scenery and many Buddhist temples, it had flourishing tea cultivation, and had been designated to produce tea cakes for the court even before the Song Dynasty.

During the reign of Emperor Song Taizong, Ding Wei was the

superintendent of imperial tea production in Fujian. A talented man of many parts, Ding Wei was good at writing poems, painting, playing chess and music, and well versed in Buddhism and Taoism. To win the emperor's favor, or a higher position and better salary, Ding Wei took a lot of trouble in creating new styles of tea cakes. During the Tang Dynasty, the cakes had a hole in the middle for a string to run through to hold them together and were roughly made. Ding Wei stopped the making of holes and designed many new patterns and dies for tea cakes.

Cai Xiang, a man of letters, and also the best calligrapher of the time, had different rules of conduct from those of Ding Wei, who liked to humor the emperor. Cai Xiang often remonstrated with the emperor, suggesting he live a simple life and show more solicitude for the ordinary people. During his two tenures of the magistracy of Fuzhou, he had done the local people a lot of good, building up seawalls, irrigating farms and planting pines for a distance of 700 *li* to protect roads. Noble and unsullied, he demonstrated the virtue of a true tea scholar. He once wrote a treatise on tea, the first part of which described the criteria for judging the quality of tea: the color, fragrance and taste. The latter part centered around teasets, especially the harmony between the colors of the sets and the tea itself. Cai Xiang also made a contribution to the production of tea cakes in the shape of dragon, which were smaller and more exquisite than earlier ones.

Differing from ordinary tea products, tea cakes in the shapes of dragons and phoenixes were full of artistry and Chinese cultural features. Besides the specially designed dragon and phoenix patterns, the dies, called *kua*, came in various shapes, such as squares, flowers, big and small dragons, and were delicately made. It was quite complicated to make such tribute tea, for the tea leaves had to be picked at dawn before the Grain Rain (6th solar term), and carefully selected, steamed, pressed, ground, caked, baked and packed before sent to the emperor. Some pattern dies, one inch in diameter, were used to make only 100 tea cakes each every year. It goes without saying such tea cakes were luxuriously packed, first in the leaves of a special kind of tree, then in layers of yellow silk, and then in red laquerware caskets with gold padlocks and official red seals, and finally in special bamboo cases. Such tribute tea, called "Bird-Tongue Budlet," could have at most three budlets on each leaf. According to contemporary records, one cake of such tea had a value of 400,000 copper coins. These expensive teas could only be enjoyed by the emperor and his empress and concubines. The officials, if they happened to be awarded one cake by the emperor, would never enjoy it but make it a present to some noble friend or worship it as a curio.

Ouyang Xiu, a celebrated literatus and statesman of the Song Dynasty, was granted only one tea cake during his twenty years of tenure of office at the imperial court; and it was almost impossible for ordinary people to have even a look at it. Such luxurious practice deviated from the spirit of tea culture and the rule of simplicity advocated by Lu Yu. But on the other hand, it demonstrated the great intelligence of the laborers who made the tea cakes.

Game Tea in the Song Dynasty

Game tea, a method in ancient China for people to value the quality of different teas in company, was well under way in the Tang Dynasty and occurred at all social strata in the Song.

Game tea first appeared in Jian'an, where the tribute tea was produced. At that time there were 1,336 official and private baking shops in the Beiyuan hills, so it was natural for game tea to be created for appraising the quality of various teas from different workshops. Fan Zhongyan, a famous man of letters of the Song, once wrote the *Song of Game Tea*, in which he described, "Before presenting the tribute tea to the emperor, tea men in the Beiyuan hills gathered to compete with each other. Baking pods scattering around, clear water from the Zhongling River boiling in cooking pots, tea dusts flying in mortars, snow-white tea foams bubbling in the cups of the tea men, the game tea was a grand view. The delicate fragrance of the tea, more pleasant than any other smell, floated in the air, greatly refreshing people's mind. When the game was set, the winner would be elated as if walking on air, and the loser feel as ashamed as a defeated soldier." The game tea soon spread to ordinary people and literati, and later even to the imperial family. *Tea and Gambling Houses*, painted by a Song artist named Liu Songnian, gave a vivid description of the scene of the game tea.

The game tea blazed a new trail for the art of tea as recorded in *The Book of Tea* by Lu Yu. Traditionally, when tea leaves were directly cooked in a pot, drinkers often sat aside to observe the changes in the tea water, meditating on the profound mystery of nature. In the Song Dynasty, however, people usually poured boiling water into cups where tea dust was placed, and stirred the water with a bamboo brush to make the tea and water completely blend with each other and foam grew like the head on a glass of beer. The person who could stir up the most and nicest foam would win. Actually what counted were the quality of the tea leaves and the skills of the competitors. In the modern Japanese tea ceremony tea is still made from dusts, but the art of making foam has been lost. In recent years, however, the Fuzhou Tea Ceremony House of China has brought this special and ancient art to light again after long-term research.

As the game tea flourished throughout the whole country, teasets, especially the cups, were given more importance by the Song people. They were fond of light-colored tea, so tea things made of black porcelain and celadon, which could better set off the tea, were highly prized.

In the view of ancient Chinese literati, the game tea relied too heavily on people's skills and lacked natural charm. They paid more attention to the environment and atmosphere of the tea ceremony. For instance, Fan Zhongyan, the great thinker of the period, liked to chant poems and play the zither in a riverside pavilion and have rare birds and ancient trees around him while cooking a pot of tea. The famous Song poet Su Dongpo thought the natural rhythm contained in tea could only be perfectly learned while collecting water from the river and cooking the tea in the wilds on a moon night when the toll from an ancient temple and the sound of the watch from the old city echoed around.

The Development of the Tea Culture in the Yuan, Ming and Qing Dynasties

Tea Culture Was Simplified in the Yuan Dynasty

The skills of tea making had taken a great leap forward in the Song Dynasty, but tea cakes in shapes of the dragon and the phoenix were too luxurious for ordinary people, and at odds with the natural qualities of tea. The Yuan Dynasty (1279-1368) was established by the Mongols, who originally were nomadic people in the north of China. In the early Yuan the Mongols could hardly agree to the exquisite culture of the Song, but with the infiltration of the Han culture and out of the need to balance their greasy diet, they gradually accepted the tea culture and simplified it. So tea cakes began to fade out, and other varieties were mass-produced, such as tender tea (similar to the modern green tea, whose tea leaves were picked in early spring), dust tea (similar to that used at the present Japanese tea ceremony) and nut tea (with additives like walnut, pine nut, sesame, apricot and chestnut). Nut tea was welcomed among ordinary people. Even today, people in Hunan and Hubei still have the habit of drinking nut tea.

In the Song Dynasty tea was used in various rites by the imperial court and upper class people, while in the Yuan period it moved closer to the everyday life of ordinary people. Actually it was representative of folk customs of the time; for instance, newly married girls showed their respect for parents-in-law and guests by presenting tea, tea was also a common subject in Song paintings, such as *The Game Tea* by Zhao Mengfu, which described the scene of game tea among ordinary people, and the unsigned *Steamed Bread and Hot Tea*, which vividly portrayed young brothers drinking tea and tasting steamed bread together. Such paintings reflect the affinity of tea with people's relationships. In a dynasty with many nationalities like Yuan, this affinity was especially important; no wonder that later tea was widely popularized.

The literati of Yuan followed their predecessors in advocating a simple and natural way of holding the tea ceremony. They usually made and drank tea in the hills, by rivers, under ancient trees and in front of thatched cottages. It was a reaction against the luxurious and difficult style of the Song Dynasty, and also a manifestation of Yuan people's wish to return to nature.

The Tea Ceremony Advocated by a Ming Prince and Ming Paintings on Tea

Established during the waning of China's feudalism, the Ming Dynasty (1368-1644) was inevitably confronted with many social problems, such as the surviving forces of the Mongols, the power struggle inside the imperial court and the peasant uprisings. The Ming rulers had to adopt a high-handed policy to consolidate their power, and the literati were the first to bear the brunt. They were forbidden to hold gatherings, and liable to be accused of opposing the court at every move. In such circumstances many intellectuals found tea a good means to express their noble aspirations and their contempt for meretricious bigwigs.

Zhu Quan, the seventeenth son of the first Ming emperor, had helped Zhu Di, the fourth son, to usurp the throne. But unfortunately the new emperor became suspicious of Zhu Quan and exiled him to the south. Feeling as depressed as the literati, Zhu Quan, a good disciple of Buddhism and Taoism, began to incline towards a reclusive life and also take a strong interest in the tea ceremony. He wrote the *Manual on Tea*, proposing the purification of people's mind by tea and advocating some reforms of the ceremonial procedures established after the abolition of tea cakes. His proposals were the basis which shaped the form and spirit of the Ming tea ceremony. The literati at the time usually burnt incense before the tea ceremony to air the room and worship heaven and earth; then they laid the table with tea things and cooked water, ground tea leaves, made tea and stirred out the bubbles with a brush. (Zhu Quan made his teapot in the shape of a Taoist alchemic vessel, and had it covered with rattan after the simple style of ancients. Later someone used bamboo, a symbol of moral integrity, as the covering.)

Many books on the tea culture appeared during the Song Dynasty. For instance, Gu Yuanqing wrote a book also named *Manual on Tea*, and Xu Xianzhong wrote *A Complete Gamut of Waters*. These books, similar to Lu Yu's *The Book of Tea*, summoned up the development of tea culture down the ages and described the new features of that in the early Ming Dynasty.

Several painters also made a contribution with their brushes to the promotion of the tea culture. For example, *The Tea Ceremony at the Huishan Hill. Lu Yu and His Tea* and *Tasting Tea* by Wen Zhengming, and *Making Tea, Playing the Zither and Tasting Tea* and *With Fragrant Green Tea* by Tang Yin vividly presented the life of leisure of the Ming literati—beside gurgling mountain springs or surging rivers, inside ancient pavilions, they played the zither and drank tea, voicing their aspirations to the green mountains and white clouds, and encouraging themselves to hold fast to their integrity in adversity.

In the later Ming, the active part in the tea ceremony waned because of the repressive policy adopted by the imperial court toward the literati. They had to move the tea ceremony into their houses, and the natural and noble qualities were gradually lost. Many new devices were added to the tea ceremony: for instance, the "100 Tea Patterns," which meant ripples of various patterns, could be stirred up in a cup of tea.

The Tea Culture Went Deep Into the Midst of Ordinary People in the Qing Dynasty

Deep penetration into ordinary people's life was the feature of the tea culture of the Qing Dynasty (1644-1911). The superb skills needed for the tea ceremony and profound spirit expressed in the tea culture were too far away from the life of ordinary people, so in the Qing period they made some adaptations. The most conspicuous one was the popularization of teahouses, where people of different social strata communicated freely with each other. As tea was welcomed by more and more people, tea things naturally became simplified, leaving the teapot and cups to play the leading role. The teaset was often called "Set of Mother and Son," because it was like a mother breast-feeding her sons when tea was poured into the cups from the pot. So the affinity that tea had with people's relationships was further strengthened.

Though the number of items needed for a set of tea things was lessened, the workmanship of them grew more excellent, especially that of the teapot. More shapes were designed, and more materials, such as purple sand, copper, porcelain, gold, silver, jade and cloisonne enamel, were developed to made the pot. At the time tea export was on a large scale, and teasets were sold abroad as incidental items. Collectors inside and outside China gradually made it a status symbol to collect Chinese teapots. Moreover, when there were foreign guests visiting China, officials got used to treating them with tea. Drinking tea, as a social custom and part of the etiquette of China, spread to other parts of the world quickly, and tea culture became a treasure of all humanity.

Chapter 3
Chinese Tea Art

The spirit of tea art and the tea ceremony is the core of Chinese tea culture. "Art" refers to the techniques and artistic process of making, cooking and tasting tea, while ceremony refers to the spirit with which the process is carried out. As tea art is visible, while the spirit is invisible, I would like to introduce tea art first.

However, before you start to learn tea art, you should first study some skills of meditation. First, close your eyes, and imagine that tea trees are growing quietly in a beautiful mountain forest under the bright sun, a soft breeze makes the branches sway, and the trees send up tender shoots. When I mention water, you will imagine vast rivers and lakes, and gurgling clear springs. The clear and sweet water will soon flow into your heart, watering your whole body, and clearing away your fatigue and worry....

Artistic Tea

"Artistic tea" means to regard the process of planting, picking, making and selecting tea as an artistic enjoyment as if reading a pure and fresh verse, or appreciating a piece of beautiful music. To Chinese, tea is a spirit in the world. When it enters your body as a drink, you will be filled with the nutrition of sunshine, the bright moon and the land, and the wonder of the whole universe.

Therefore, all the famous Chinese tea culture experts have had the experience of planting, picking and making tea by themselves, or learning the spirit of the labor from tea growers. Lu Yu, the founder of Chinese tea culture, traveled all over the areas along the Yangtze River and Taihu Lake, and clambered up tier upon tier of cliffs. He put up for the night at ancient Taoist temples or the homes of tea growers in the villages. Through such practice, he understood tea's characteristics more profoundly, and threw himself into picking and making tea.

Tea growers should first select the right places to plant tea trees. The best tea is grown on the sand and soil on mountains; the second-class, on humus soil; and the low-grade, on loess. Wild tea trees are better than planted ones. Purple tea-leaves are the best, while green ones are inferior; those curling like bamboo shoots are better than the pointed or unfolding ones. Tea trees usually grow on the northern slopes of hills with moderate rain and sunshine. Therefore, most of the growing areas of famous teas are very beautiful. Lu Yu evaluated the 31 tea-growing prefectures of the Tang Dynasty, of which eight were in Sichuan Province, according to this standard. The second largest tea growing area was around the Taihu Lake, which was most famous for "Gu Zhu Purple Bamboo Shoots." The Taihu Lake, with its vast expanse of misty, rolling waters, clear springs, and surrounded by beautiful mountain forests, had suitable climate and soil for growing tea. Lu Yu wrote *The Book of Tea* on the Zhushan Mountain, south of the Taihu Lake. He also built a house in Shangrao, west of Taihu Lake. Tea produced in Sichuan, Zhejiang and Jiangxi provinces and the Wuyi Mountain in Fujian Province, is still very famous. During the Song Dynasty, people thought highly of Jianzhou tea produced in Fujian Province, and many tea growers went deep into the mountains to look for famous tea. During the Ming Dynasty, people loved Wuyi tea. With its cavernous and serene mountain roads and magnificent scenery, Mount Wuyi attracted many tea growers to go into the mountain to look for tea each year, and some of them even persisted in doing so for 60 years. Some tea growers built villas in the Bright Moon Gorge of Mount Wuyi, and planted various tea to evaluate them. They studied tea from childhood to old age, and finally grasped its deepest principles. Zhuang Zi, one of the founders of Chinese Taoism, believed that only the things which agreed with natural laws were really excellent and beautiful. The whole process of Chinese tea art reflects this conception of nature.

The picking time of tea is very important. It was not very strict during the Tang Dynasty. It could be February, March and April by the lunar calendar. (The old Chinese calendar is lunisolar calendar, which not only paid attention to the waxing and waning of the moon, but also gave consideration to solar terms, and the length of years and months as determined by astronomical phenomena. The 24 solar terms are also called the lunar calendar, because they are significant for agricultural production. A lunar month will occur more than a month later than that of the Gregorian calendar.) The picking time became very strict in the Song Dynasty. The best time was usually between the Waking of Insects (one of the 24 solar terms, beginning from around March 6 by the Gregorian calendar, when the weather is becoming warmer, and the hibernating animals are about to come up out of the ground to move about) and Pure Brightness (one of the 24 solar terms, beginning around April 5 by the Gregorian calendar, when the cold weather and withered and yellow grass and trees are replaced by warm weather and luxuriant grass and trees). It is best to plant tea trees in the early hours of sunny days, when morning dews have not dispersed. After the sun rises, the cream of the tea will be exhausted, and its moisture content affected. Tea is picked with the nails instead of the fingers so that its quality is not affected by the hands' temperature. The hands' movements of the picking tea women are like beautiful

31

dance movements. Tea's grade can be judged by the shapes and tenderness of tea buds. Generally speaking, the tenderer the better. A single bud looks like a lotus flower which has just come into bloom, so it is called "lotus stamen;" two buds, like the red tassels of ancient spears, "chess spears;" three buds, like a bird opening its mouth and sticking out its tongue, "sparrow's tongue." The beautiful names stimulate people's affection, so they have a beautiful and peaceful feeling before entering teahouses.

The process of making tea is also an artistic procedure. In the Tang Dynasty, there were four varieties of tea: weak tea, loose tea, tea dust and tea cakes. Weak tea was similar to modern brick tea, which could be restored and transported easily, but it was not of high quality. Loose tea, which was similar to the modern loose tea, would be collected right after being cured. Tea dust was ground into fine powder for the sake of convenience. The three above-mentioned varieties were used by people in their daily lives, while Lu Yu mainly introduced tea cakes, which reflected tea art. In the Song Dynasty, eight cakes of Great Dragon tea equaled one *jin*, which was rather heavy, while Little Dragon tea, twelve cakes for one jin, was exquisitely shaped: some were square, some looked like six-petal plum blossoms, and some like elongated pointed jade tablets which were held in the hands of ancient rulers on ceremonial occasions). They were also decorated with various designs such as dragons, phoenixes and auspicious clouds, and they reflected many human factors.

Water

Now, let's talk about the relationship between water and tea art. Please imagine gurgling springs, the waves of rivers, misty vast lakes, and sweet and clear well water.

The relationship between water and tea is similar to that between wine and water. All wine experts understand that excellent water quality is essential for the best wine, while tea art is even stricter with water. It is impossible to make fragrant tea without good water. Therefore, famous tea experts are all proficient in distinguishing water. According to Xu Cishu, a tea expert of the Ming Dynasty, tea's finest qualities can be brought into play with the help of water; therefore, it is impossible to make excellent tea without good water. Zhang Dafu, a tea expert of the Qing Dynasty, even regarded the water as more important than tea. He believed that a cup of excellent tea contained 20 percent tea and 80 percent water. If you could not taste the flavor of a good tea, probably it was because of the poor water quality.

Lu Yu discussed tea water exhaustively in *the Book of Tea*. According to him, the water used to brew tea should be different from ordinary drinking water. Water from mountains was the best, river water was inferior, and well water was low grade. The water from mountain springs was better than that from waterfalls. The water from mountains would become undrinkable if it was stored in valleys for a long time, because there would be many insects and germs in the water. Therefore, tea water should be drawn from clear flowing water in sparsely populated areas. Dew drops from mountain stalactites, clear flowing springs and clear river streams were regarded as the sources of the best water for brewing tea. This principle is also reasonable from the modern scientific point of view. Zhang Youxin, a tea expert of the Tang Dynasty, wrote the *Notes on Brewing Tea* according to Lu Yu's experience. He listed nearly 20 famous varieties of water suitable for brewing tea, arranged in the order of their quality. They were:

The Kangwanggu Valley Spray of the Lushan Mountain in Jiangzhou; Huishan Mountain Spring in Wuxi of Changzhou; Lanxi Mountain Spring in Qizhou; the frog-shaped river in the fan-shaped valley in Xiazhou; Huqiu Temple Spring on the Tiger Hill in Suzhou; the pool under the Stone Bridge of the Zhaoxian Temple on the Lushan Mountain in Jiangzhou; Lingshui Lake of the Yangtze River in Yangzhou; West Hills Waterfall in Hongzhou; Huaishui River Source in Tongbai County of Tangzhou, Dinglong Spring on the Lushan Mountain in Jiangzhou; Avalokitesvara Temple Well in Danyang County of Runzhou; Lingshui Lake in the upper reaches of the Hanjiang River; Chunxi Brook in the Yuxu Cave in Guizhou; West Valley Spray in Wuguan of Shangzhou; the Wusongjiang River in Suzhou; Southern Peak Waterfall on the Heavenly-Terrace Mountain in Zhaozhou; Binzhou Garden Spring; Yanling Beach in Tonglu of Yanzhou; and snow water.

Later generations are doubtful about whether these varieties of water were evaluated by Lu Yu. For example, the 16th source on the list was a waterfall, while Lu Yu opposed the brewing of tea with waterfall water. Zhang Youxin attached great importance to water, which promoted the further study of water quality. However, it seems unnecessary to arrange the sources in order, because various waters are suitable for brewing various teas, and everyone has his own taste. However, water experts of past dynasties shared a lot in common in their evaluation of tea water, stressing sweet and light flowing water with clean sources.

Emperor Qian Long of the Qing Dynasty (1736-1796) had not only a head for politics, but also deep love for Chinese traditional culture. He was keen on tea culture, and had original views on water quality because he had traveled extensively. He would weigh it with a special little silver *dou* whenever he found excellent water. Finally, he concluded that water from the Jade Spring Hill in Beijing's western suburbs and the Yixun River beyond the Great Wall was the lightest, while water from the Pearl Spring in Jinan and the Gold Hill Spring on the Yangtze River bank ranked second and third, respectively.

Tea experts of past dynasties had different understandings of water, and they arranged famous water in different orders. We cannot determine who is right, because the natural environment changes constantly, the quality of water in the same place can change over time. Lu Xing, a tea expert, put forward an important principle—tea art cannot do without high-quality water. Some experts believed that it was unnecessary to brew tea with famous water, and people could get qualified water in all places. They held that people should learn to "cultivate water" in the light of local conditions. For example, water from the Yangtze River should be taken at midnight from the upper or middle reaches with their excellent vegetation, and quiet and secluded environment. Some people take water from the first snow, morning dews and light drizzle. Drizzle water should be caught with utensils in the open before it falls to the ground, so it is called "rootless water." In ancient times, when air pollution was not serious, water vapor rose from the ground to the air and became rain or snow after being purified naturally, so the water was clean. At the same time, this method of taking water also implied the linkage of tea with the universal spirit. As far back as the Han Dynasty, Emperor Han Wu Di had a bronze statue of an "immortal catching dews." Today, there is still such a bronze statue in Beihai Park in Beijing—an immortal holding a plate high to catch rain and dew from heaven. The viewpoints of the Chinese tea culture experts fully reflected Taoist ideologies of absorbing the ultimate in nature in order to serve people, and seek natural beauty.

Teasets

As the old Chinese idiom goes, "it is necessary to have effective tools to do good work." It refers to ordinary labor and creations. As a material activity, tea art is also a spiritual and artistic creation; therefore teasets should not only be convenient to use, but also show orderliness and aesthetic feeling in their arrangement, combination and operation. Lu Yu designed 24 vessels when he created Chinese tea art, which were recorded in *the Book of Tea*. The "24 vessels", as shown in the pictures, included:

1. Wind stove: Used to make a fire to brew tea. It was designed in accordance with Taoist five-elements theory, and Confucian etiquette and spirit, and was usually cast in iron in ancient times, while later some were made of sintered mud.

2. Bamboo basket: A square basket woven in bamboo filigree used to pick tea. Ancient tea devotees attached great importance to actual practice, and usually picked, baked and processed tea by themselves before drinking.

3. Charcoal seizor: The ancients used charcoal to brew tea, and believed that tea's quality would vary with the type of fire. The Charcoal seizer was a one-*chi*-long ironware with six ridges used to break charcoal pieces.

4. Fire-clip: Used to grip charcoal pieces to put it into a stove.

5. Boiler: Used to brew tea. The boiler has been retained in Japanese tea ceremonies up to the present. It was made of iron or stone in the Tang Dynasty, but some rich families used silver boilers.

6. Wooden stand: To place a boiler with a stove underneath. During the Ming and Qing dynasties, mud stoves were wrapped with rattan and bamboo so wooden stands became unnecessary.

7. Paper bag: To keep brewed tea so that the fragrance would not be let out.

8. Tea roller and tea dust cleaner: The former was used to grind tea, and the latter, to clean tea dust off the roller. We can see the original shape of the tea roller among the teasets unearthed in the Temple of Dharma Gate in Shaanxi Province. It was composed of a rectangular mill groove and a turbine with an axle.

9. Tea basket: To sift tea.

10. *Ze*: It was like a pancake-shaped soup spoon, and was used to measure tea.

11. Water container: To store unboiled water.

12. Filter bag: To filter tea water. It was made of copper, wood or bamboo.

13. Gourd ladle: To ladle out water. Sometimes it was replaced by a wooden dipper.

14. Bamboo clip: To stir tea water to give full play to tea's properties.

15. Salt stand: To hold salt powder. In the Tang Dynasty, people used salt as a seasoning while drinking tea.

16. Processed jar: To store hot water. People in the Tang Dynasty stressed three key points when brewing tea. When the water boils for the first time, put tea into the boiler to brew it directly; the second time, ladle out foams and put it into the processed jar; the third time, pour the boiled water from the jar into the boiler.

17. Bowls: Necessary implements for tasting tea.

18. *Ben*: To store bowls.

19. *Zha*: To wash the vessels. It was similar to a pot-scouring brush.

20. Water collector: To store water.

21. Dregs collector: To gather tea dregs.

22. Cloth: To clean the vessels.

23. Teaset stand: To display a teaset. It was similar to a modern tea table or wine stand.

24. Big basket: To store all the vessels after drinking tea.

It seems hard for modern people to understand that such complicated vessels had to be used to drink tea. However, they were necessities for the ancients to perform and perfect the ritual of drinking tea. A person could also change his mood and temper his

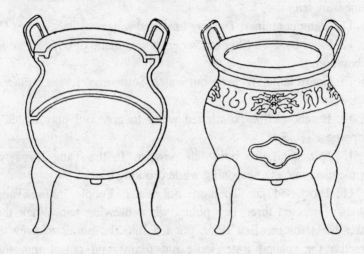

Wind stove

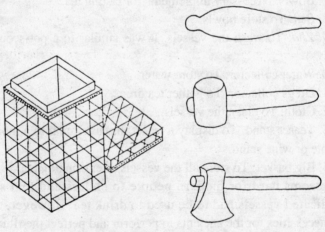

Bamboo basket   Charcoal seizor

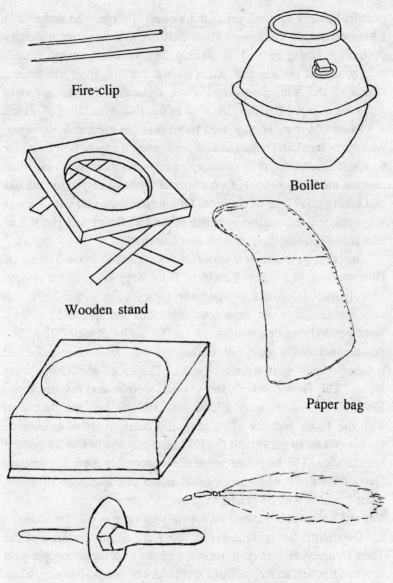

Fire-clip

Boiler

Wooden stand

Paper bag

Tea roller and tea dust cleaner

practical ability through using the vessels. People who understand Chinese cooking culture all know that the system of meticulously designing, arranging and combining, and rationally using vessels was practiced on a grand scale, as we can see from the bronze wares of the Yin, Shang and Zhou dynasties. It was not only reflected in royal families, but also in the folk wine ritual in which a 70-year-old man/woman used more *jues* (an ancient wine vessel with three legs) and *dous* (an ancient stemmed cup or bowl, similar to a standing plate) than ordinary family members. Such customs showed the Chinese people's traditional virtue of respecting the old and taking good care of children. Of course, compared with ancient wine culture, tea culture is richer in natural flavor and the joy of life. However, they both stress order and rhythm.

In recent years, several teasets were unearthed in the Temple of Dharma Gate in Shaanxi Province. They were given to the temple as a charitable donation by Emperor Tang Xi Zong (873-889); and they were so exquisite, ingenious, luxurious and splendid that they went beyond the descriptions in Lu Yu's *The Book of Tea*. The vessels included a tea roller, basket, *ze*, salt stand, chopsticks and bowls. Some of them were carved with Emperor Tang Xizong's pet name, "The Fifth Brother", the vessels' weight, and manufacturer. Most of the teasets were gilded with silverwares, and decorated with the Taoist patterns of an immortal riding a crane, auspicious clouds and swan geese, and the Buddhist patterns of Datura and the lotus design. The exquisite vessels won people's great admiration. One of them, an olive-green bowl made of "Porcelain of secret color," which was as bright as glass, is a rare ancient chinaware. Various beautiful colors would appear when it was filled with tea.

During the Song Dynasty, teasets were similar to those of the Tang Dynasty. However, to meet the needs of contests, people paid special attention to the qualities and colors of bowls. Because white tea was popular and contestants had to beat white foams, special

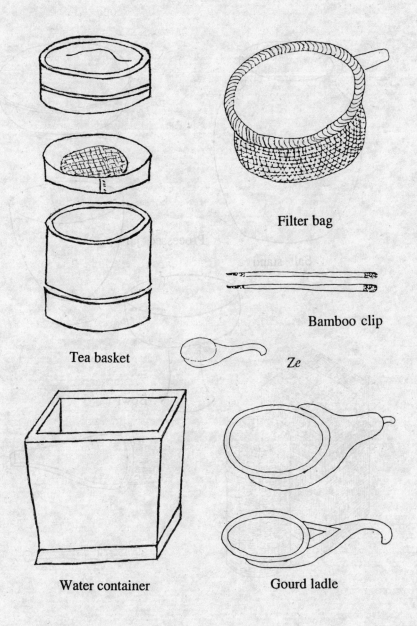

Filter bag

Bamboo clip

Tea basket

Ze

Water container

Gourd ladle

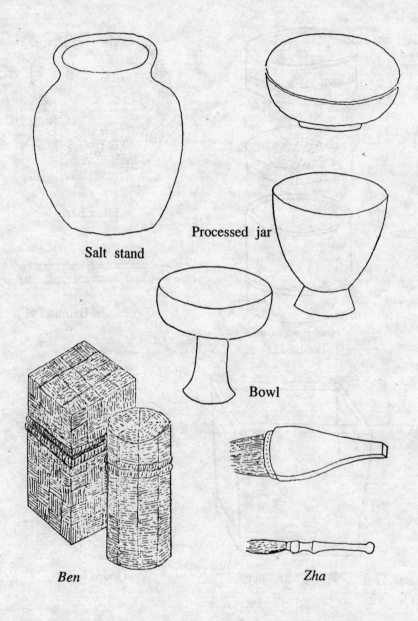

Salt stand

Processed jar

Bowl

Ben

Zha

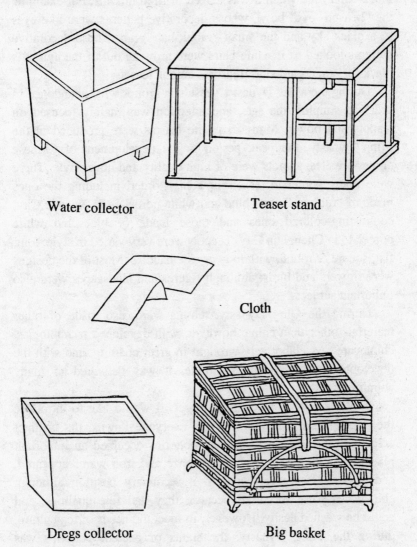

Water collector

Teaset stand

Cloth

Dregs collector

Big basket

attention was paid to black and celadon wares to set off the tea to advantage. Special natural decorative patterns appeared on some black chinaware when it was glazed or fired in kilns. For example, the "heaven- eye" bowl, whose decorative patterns were like eyes in a black sky and the small "rabbit-hair" cup, whose decorative patterns looked as if white hairs were growing out of the animal's black fur, are regarded as treasures among teasets.

During the Ming Dynasty, vessels in groups were abandoned in order to simplify the sets, and attention was mainly focused on teapots and bowls. Many exquisite teasets were produced in the Ming Dynasty, the peak period in the development of Chinese chinaware. The teapots were of high quality and novel style. There were many porcelain teasets of a high order, including the ones made of "ruby red", and blue and white porcelain in Xuande City, contrasting-colored ones and those made of blue and white porcelain in Chenghua City. Teapots were very varied in style: long, flat, square or round, with loop or side handles. Most of the designs were flowers and birds, although figures and landscapes were also important subjects.

During the Qing Dynasty, teasets were also made of other materials other than china; however, with developed technologies, chinaware was elaborately wrought in great quantity, and with the development of international trade, it was delivered to many countries.

Into this history of Chinese teasets, I would like to introduce the purple sand porcelain pot. As everyone kowns, the brilliant achievements of Chinese ancient potteries occupied an important place in cooking culture. Later, bronze and iron wares appeared, and potteries were relegated to a secondary position although chinawares were still used because they had fine qualities, and could be washed easily. However, to meet the needs of tea culture, during the Ming Dynasty, the status of ancient potteries was

44

improved. After teasets in groups were abandoned, people made tea in teapots directly. It took a long time to make fermented and semi-fermented tea. China teapots were so impermeable that the tea would spoil if kept too long in them. The purple sand pottery pot was invented to solve this problem. It was made of special clay from Yixing, Xianyang, Chaozhou and some other cities. It became bronze in color after being sintered. In the Ming Dynasty, an excellent purple sand teapot was equal to the wealth of a middle-class family, so you can see that it was very valuable. At the time, some people were so fond of exquisite purple sand teapots that they tried all means to collect them, even, in some cases, dissipating their fortune. This common practice was continued until the Qing Dynasty. Purple sand teapots have always been treasured by collectors.

Why are they treasured so much? On one hand, they make tea, especially fermented tea, send forth its full fragrance. Pottery clay absorbs fragrance easily, so an excellent purple sand teapot is full of tea's essence after it has been used for a long time, and will send forth a refreshing fragrance immediately when people used it. On the other hand, the teapots, accord with the requirements of tea culture. The Chinese people always advocate primitive simplicity and naturalness. Purple sand teapots impart a sense of natural beauty, and give people a feeling of moderation when they hold them in both hands. The effect is in concord with the restful charm required by tea culture in both vision and somesthesia.

The purple sand teapot is also treasured because of the artistic designs of the manufacturers. There were many experts in purple sand teapots. The teapot was first invented by an eminent monk of the Gold Sand Temple who remained anonymous. However, for all practical purposes, its real originator was Gong Chun, and the teapot invented by him was called the Gongchun Teapot. Gong Chun was a boy serving in a scholar's study, and was well-trained in accomplishments and practical spirituality. He was greatly influenced by Buddhism because he lived in the Golden Sand Temple at the time he tried to make the teapot. The formation of his unique artistic style may be attributed to many factors. His works were very simple and elegant in color and shape, and were lively and diverse in style: some looked like red melons full of the fragrance of earth; some were like tree stumps, which looked like old men telling the long history of tea; some were like fragrant buds, which naturally suited tea.

Shi Dabin, an expert succeeding Gong Chun, often visited the Songjiang River. He had close contact with Chen Jiru, a famous tea expert of the Ming Dynasty, and absorbed Chen's ideas on tea culture. The design of his works was ingeniously conceived. For example, a small teapot looked like a monk's cap, which naturally reminded one of a monk praying to Buddha in the ancient temple. The message was clear: you drink tea to purify your soul, and the teapot could bring you immediately to Buddhism's realm.

Brewing and Tasting Tea

The methods of drinking tea has changed several times since the Han and Tang dynasties. The general methods are described below.

1. Brewing tea:

The tea dust is brewed directly in teapots. This method was most popular before the Tang Dynasty. Lu Yu introduces the whole process in detail in *the Book of Tea*. First, grind the tea cakes into dust with a tea roller, then pour choice water into a teapot. Brew it on a charcoal fire, and add the tea dust when the water is almost boiling. The tea and water would blend with each other. Foam appears when the water boils for the second time; the foam is called *bomo*. Lu Yu regarded it as the cream of tea, which should be ladled out and kept in an inert jar. Tea and water further blend together, and waves appear when the water boils for the third time; *bomo* is then added to the teapot. The resulting liquid is called *Jiufei* or *Yuhua*. When the cream becomes even, the tea is ready to serve.

2. Dripping tea:

This method came into being in the Tang Dynasty, and became popular in the Song Dynasty, when people did not brew tea in teapots. Grind teacakes into powder, and then make the tea in bowls with gently boiling water. The tea and water should also blend, so special attention should be paid to the teapot brush, the utensil for stirring tea. Most of the brushes are made of bamboo, although they can also be made of iron, silver and gold. The quality and quantity of foam is determined by the brush's shape and one's stirring skill. Pour the water into a tea bowl, and strike the bowl hard with the brush. Tea and water would blend, and *bomo* would appear gradually, looking like piles of white clouds or snow. The quality of tea should be judged by whether foam appears soon and water waves appear late. A tea with white foam, and its water waves appearing late without dispersing is regarded as the top-grade one, and tea devotees determine victory accordingly. It has been recorded that the tea foam stirred by a tea devotee of the Song Dynasty looked like white clouds or snow piling above the bowl. In recent years, tea enthusiasts have been studying this method, and they can also make foam rise above the bowls, but the foam is not like clouds, and caves in the middle. This might due to the shape of the teapot brush and the method of stirring tea, which are different from those of the ancients. The present Japanese tea ceremony also adopts this method. However, the tea dust is fine enough, and the stirring force is not strong enough. As a result, green tea only looks like green flecks floating on the water.

3. Dripping flower tea:

This method was created by Zhu Quan in the Ming Dynasty. The tea made this way had special fragrance and artistic effect. Put the buds of plum blossoms, sweet-scented osmanthus and jasmine together with tea dust into a bowl, and speed the opening of the buds with steam. You may enjoy its color, fragrance and taste simultaneously, and it is also a feast for the eyes.

4. Semi-made tea:

Add walnuts, melon seeds, pine nuts and other dry fruits to the tea, and pour hot water. Tea enthusiasts used to enjoy themselves by picking, brewing and drinking semi-made tea on mountains and plains.

5. Made tea:

This well-known method has been used from the Ming and Qing dynasties to the present. Although it is simple and convenient, great differences exist between various regions and varieties of tea. It takes different times to make red tea (known as black tea in the west), green tea and scented tea, and their optimum water temperatures are also different. Green tea is delicate, so the water temperature should not be high. For example, *longjing* tea would become tasteless after pouring hot water on it two or three times. Red tea is hard, and the blades are thick, so it takes a longer time to make it. Scented tea requires moderate temperature and time. People who really understand tea would not only make tea to drink; they would first appreciate the shape of the tea, and determine its variety and production area by appearance and smell. Various teas have different shapes. *Longjing* dried tea is elongated, pekoe is needle-shaped, and pearl tea looks like round peals. Their appearance in the water is also different. Some look like green vines hanging upside down, and some falls to the water bottom. For example, hirtellous clover-shrub root looks like a golden ring, while *Huangjingui* is orange, and looks like gold.

The made tea method requires one to pour skillfully. Tea makers with excellent skills can go the rounds, pouring the tea evenly from a teapot into a dozen cups on a plate without any spillage.

As an art, tea-drinking requires a special environment. In ancient times there were many participants in large tea parties and imperial tea feasts. For example, emperors Kang Xi and Qian Long of the Qing Dynasty held top-grade tea feasts in the Hall of Supreme Harmony in the Forbidden City, and there were thousands of participants at each feast. However, according to the theory of traditional Chinese tea ceremony, it is unnecessary to have very many participants. The theory required one to drink tea in elegant environment, such as by clear springs or in bamboo groves on mountains, in ancient temples and small pavilions, or in one's own garden while appreciating flowers, snow or fish. Many artists of the Ming Dynasty painted such environments. For example, the painting *Tasting Tea* drawn by Tang Yin depicts some tea devotees drinking tea in a bright hay-thatched hall surrounded by ancient trees and a growth of green plants under bamboo fences on a lofty green mountain. In the Ming Dynasty, most tea enthusiasts built teahouses in their own courtyards and villas. They would burn incense to purify the air in the room, and wash all the teasets before drinking, and then invite friends to drink tea while writing poems, painting or having a long talk under the moon. Generally speaking, the tea's quality, the drinkers' moral quality and the environment should harmonize. People could let nature take its course while a whole family or a couple drink tea at home. Li Qingzhao, a female *ci* poet of the Song Dynasty, liked drinking tea. Most of her popular verses were miserable, sad and gloomy. However, she had a good and perfect family when she was young. The couple often drank tea while writing poems, and the verses written by her at that time were full of happiness. Her husband Zhao Mingcheng was an epigraphist, and was of great attainment in his appreciation of ancient utensils, but he could not compare with Li Qingzhao in drinking tea and writing poems. Li often burst with laughing, and even spilled the tea in her mouth onto her clothes, an action which did not agree with feudal custom. Tea devotees advocated drinking tea in a natural and harmonious environment.

Chapter 4
The Spirit of Chinese Tea Ceremony

People who have watched a performance of the Japanese tea ceremony often ask: Why is it called tea ceremony in Japan and tea art in China? Is it because China has no tea ceremony, or that the Chinese performance is not as qualified as the Japanese one? In fact, the order is reversed. A Japanese friend of tea culture circles said, "China is the birthplace of the tea ceremony. One of her children ran to Japan, and achieved gratifying results." The words are correct, for the tea ceremony really orginates in China. The questions arise because of a lack of knowledge about the development of tea culture, but also because of the different understanding of "*dao*" among the Chinese and Japanese. According to the Chinese, "*dao*" is the nature, origin and law of a thing. "The Way of Nature is invisible," so the Chinese do not name a thing "*dao*" easily. To the Japanese, "*dao*" means skills: flower arrangement is called "flower way," and wrestling is called "judo." As a cultural activity, tea performance is also called "*dao*." We Chinese people believe that the artistic process of drinking tea is merely a form, which tends to be superficial, while the intent is to express the inner spirit. We also regard tea art and tea ceremony as different aspects of a problem. Tea art is a visible material activity, but only if spiritual force is aroused in the process can it be called *dao*. Therefore, I believe that the core of tea culture is the "visible art and invisible *dao*." In fact, Lu Yu, the Saint of Tea

Culture, and other experts of the past dynasties manifested the spirit through the process of tea culture. To explain it more clearly, I would like to introduce the spiritual concepts first.

The spirit of Chinese tea ceremony is a broad and profound system absorbing the cream of Confucian, Taoist and Buddhist thought which fully demonstrates the Chinese traditional idea of the close integration and interaction of the material and the spiritual.

Confucian Thoughts and the Spirit of Chinese Tea Ceremony

Each nation has its own unique cultural system and individual characteristics. Great differences exist in the orientation of culture and values between the East and West. The West advocates fire and power, while China is characterized as peaceful, gentle and kind, firm and tenacious. These qualities are fully shown in the golden mean and harmony, the characteristics of Confucian thought. Tea, which is gentle and peaceful, accords with these characteristics. Though Taoism and Buddhism have played important roles in the development of tea culture, Confucian thought is regarded as the core of the spirit of Chinese tea ceremony, which is demonstrated in the following four aspects.

Tea's Gentle and Peaceful Characters Embody the Golden Mean of the Confucian School

It is said that Westerners are open and enthusiastic, and their dispositions are like wine, while we Easterners, sober, sensible, gentle and enduring, are like tea. We also advocate getting along with each other in a friendly and harmonious way. Therefore, Westerners stress individual struggle; easterners, collectivism.

Eastern attributes in Chinese tea culture prominently reflects. We should get along with each other just as man and nature should be in harmony. The Confucianists introduced this thought into tea ceremony, advocating the creation of a harmonious atmosphere through the drinking of tea. The characteristics of tea and water are similar: though it seems to be delicate, water is very magnanimous; though tea is only an ordinary drink, people will learn to be tolerant and understanding through drinking it. Therefore, in ancient times, imperial courts entertained foreign envoys with tea, while in modern times, people still offer tea to guests to express their friendliness and to strengthen solidarity. In China, tea parties are held in institutions and factories at the end of a year. At these parties, managers drink tea together with staff, and have heart-to-heart talks to get to know each other's viewpoints better and to express their solicitude and understanding. Many disagreements can be solved at such parties.

The Confucianists advocated the golden mean: that is, people should approach problems from all angles so as not to go to extremes. The mean was highlighted in tea culture. Although water and fire seem to be incompatible, Lu Yu stressed their unitarity. How could one boil water without fire? And how could a person make tea without water? Therefore, Lu Yu moulded wind animals, firebirds, fish and water on teapots, showing the unitarity of wind, fire and water. Fire is fanned by wind, water boiled by fire, and tea brewed by water. Lu Yu's viewpoint originated from the *Book of Changes*—"first of the five books." According to it, wind was *xun* (☴); fire, *li* (☲); and water, *kan* (☵). The fire could only burn vigorously when wind blew under the teapot. *Xun* and *li* were jointly called *ding* (䷱), which could brew food and drink. Fire and water were jointly called *jiji* (䷾), expressing the idea that everything was ready. Fire rises while water falls. However, Chinese people exchange their positions. Our social ideal is to realize universal harmony in the world; Nature is made up of gold, wood, water, fire and earth, which are called "the five elements," and "harmonious five elements" is our conception of nature. Lu Yu advocated tea culture, and believed that the state would be unified only if people got along with each other harmoniously, and diseases would be eliminated only if the five elements were harmonious.

Under the guidance of such thoughts, the spirit of solidarity and harmony is carried out in each link of tea culture. The *Painting of 100 Children* drawn by Su Hanchen depicted 100 lovely children drinking tea while playing, symbolizing that all Chinese ethnic groups get along with each other. Tea experts express the thought through a tea set. People call teapot "tea mother," and teacups, "tea son," showing that our motherland cares for each of her children. In the Qing Dynasty, Chen Mingyuan made a teapot, whose body was made of the tightly-bounded roots of three old trees. The teapot shared three roots, a pot of water and a lid, expressing the idea that "it is impossible to break 10 pairs of chopsticks simultaneously," and that all ethnic groups of China were linked together by the same root. The Chinese regard it as the spirit of tea culture that man's nature is good at birth. People all over the world may draw inspiration from tea culture to improve their relations.

Chinese Tea Ceremony Is a Happy Cultural Activity

The Japanese tea ceremony mainly absorbed the elements of Buddhist thought in Chinese tea culture, and stressed bitterness and quietness. Chinese tea culture, however, is full of happiness, for it fully absorbed the magnanimous Confucian outlook on life.

The Chinese believe in pantheism, and regard all mortals that have made contributions to mankind as gods after they die. In other words, Chinese gods are phantoms of mortals, so we believe in the self-perpetuating strength of mankind. As history continues, we should place our hopes on the later generations to fulfill unaccomplished aims. We are always confident in the future, and have a deep love for life. Therefore, in the Chinese tea ceremony, imperial concubines and princesses in the imperial palace could drink tea while appreciating music; scholar, drink tea while playing musical instruments, painting, chanting poems or appreciating beautiful natural scenery. Tea-drinking was also a happy family occasion. Even monks took pleasure in drinking tea. Jiao Ran, a famous monk of the Tang Dynasty, who was a friend of Lu Yu, helped to ceate Chinese tea culture with Lu Yu and other scholars. Instead of stressing strict ascetic practices, he advocated drinking tea while appreciating fragrant flowers, the bright moon and beautiful music, which was full of the human touch. He was also a famous poet, and often composed poems in reply to friends at tea parties.

The Chinese believe that bitterness will not last long, and creates an excellent opportunity for people to temper themselves. As nature is always in motion, and human life goes on without end, we should be optimistic. We drink tea to develop our vital spirit, and help others generously. The melody of the spirit of Chinese tea ceremony is composed of the sober, optimistic, enthusiastic, connected and tolerant spirit of the Confucian School.

Cultivate One's Honesty, Elegant Taste and Active Attitude Towards Life with the Spirit of Tea

Some people misunderstood tea as a time-killer for idlers and hermits. During the Ming and Qing dynasties, many tea connoisseurs were pessimistic. At the end of the Qing Dynasty, people of the "Eight Banners" regarded tea as a plaything. However, one can realize that the active Confucian spirit has been the main trend of tea culture if he takes a panoramic view of the history of tea culture. Chinese intellectuals have a strong sense of responsibility and vocation, and always "regard it as their own responsibility to concern themselves with world affairs," and "plead for the people." Chinese tea culture absorbed this fine tradition. As far back as the Eastern and Western Jin, and the Southern dynasties, Lu Na, Huan Wen and several other politicians created the early tea culture, advocating the cultivation of one's honesty with tea. Idle talkers commented freely worldly affairs while drinking tea. Lu Yu formally created the system of Chinese tea culture in the Tang Dynasty, synthesizing Confucian, Taoist and Buddhist thought, with the Confucian active attitude towards life as the guiding principle. Lu Yu was concerned about his country and his people. The chaos caused by the rebel leader, An Lushan, had just been put down when Lu Yu made tea stoves. He was taking refuge in Huzhou City and the good tidings that the country had become stable filled him with joy. He carved the words: "made in the Ming Reign when the Great Tang defeated *Hu*" on the stoves. Yan Zhenqing, with whom he studied tea culture, was a famous calligrapher and politician. An Lushan launched armed rebellions in the north, and soon led his troops to the south. The prefectures of Hebei fell successively; only Yan Zhenqing kept Pingyuan Prefecture, as his battle field. When he was the Minister of the Ministry of Punishment, he offended the emperor and prime minister by using blunt words to remonstrate with them, and was demoted to Huzhou City, where he became acquainted with Lu Yu. We can see, therefore, the founders of tea culture all had a strong sense of responsibility to their country and people. The boiler made by Lu Yu had a square handle, symbolizing honesty; wide edges, lofty ideals; and a long lower part, the golden mean. Most of the tea connoisseurs maintained the fine tradition of reflecting the principles of administering a country through specific tea sets. In the middle and later periods of the Ming Dynasty, most of the emperors were fatuous and self-indulgent; the tea connoisseurs therefore paid special attention to cultivating integrity by not associating themselves with undesirable elements. They wrapped stoves with bamboo and called them *kujiejun* (Mr. Painstaking Integrity), suggesting that they would learn from the progressive quality of bamboo. The steelyard used for measuring tea was called *zhiquan*. *Quan* was a part of an ancient weighing apparatus—the sliding weight of a steelyard. One small teaset showed the standard of measuring right and wrong, indicating that tea connoisseurs could distinguish truth from falsehood. Confucianists encourages the cultivation of one's moral character and putting one's family affairs in order, and then administering state affairs. However, instead of always keeping a straight face to show concern about the country, one should "alternate tension with relaxation, which was the principle of kings Wen and Wu." Therefore, it should not be regarded as negative behavior for some tea connoisseurs to have brewed and sample tea in the wilderness.

Tea Ceremony Served as a Rite

China has always been known as a land of propriety and righteousness. Modern people often mistake the rite system for the social estate system. Confucian rites not only restrained people's behavior and established social order, but they also implied mutual respect and care and the virtues of showing respect for the aged and love for the young, the comity between brothers, respect for teachers and love for students. People become sober and sensible through drinking tea, and as a result, they can carry out the spirit of the rites easily.

Tea was first served during rites in the Song Dynasty. At that time, the tea ceremony was used on the grand feasts held by the court in spring and autumn. The details were recorded in the

History of the Song Dynasty. Tea would be "granted" when imperial competitive examinations were held, when the emperor interviewed officials and received foreign envoys, and on the memorial ceremonies of various holidays. Ethnic minorities were also affected by the system. At first, the State of Liao and Song imperial court confronted each other, and fought many battles. According to the treaty concluded after they became sworn brothers at Tanyuan Pool, they sent envoys to each other. A tea ceremony was held when the Song imperial court received the envoy from the State of Liao, and also at a send-off party. Though the State of Liao was founded by Qidan, the nomandic people, they appreciated the rite system of the Song Dynasty. Many details about the tea ceremonies held on the birthdays of the emperor and queen mother, when offering a sacrifice to mountains, worshipping the sun, or on other important occasions were recorded in the *History of the State of Liao.*

According to Volume 115 of the *History of the Song Dynasty,* when a prince took an imperial concubine, he had to offer 100 *jin* of tea and other presents. Later, it became customary to hold tea ceremonies at weddings. The rites of tea-drinking originated from Buddhism, which later affected families and society. The *Family Rites* written by Qiu Jun in the Ming Dynasty provided the details of tea ceremony, which greatly affected the common people, and spread to Korea. South Korea has paid great attention to tea ceremony even to today.

The Spirit of Taoist Tea Culture

The social influence of Chinese tea culture is mainly reflected in Confucian thought, while its aesthetic viewpoint, skills and practical spirit are mainly influenced by Taoist thought.

The Taoist School and Taoism are entirely different. The Taoist School appeared much earlier than Confucian thought. The spirit of Confucian thought focused on administering the society, while Taoist thought stressed the relationship between man and nature. Lao Zi, the founder of Taoist thought, was born in the State of Chu more than 2700 years ago. No one knew how many years he had lived—some people say 200 years, while some even say 600 years. Lao Zi advocated looking at things dialectically, and stressed that people should see the reverse as well as the obverse side of things. For example, when others said firmness was better than softness, he would retort that one's teeth were firm, but they would drop out before he died; while the tongue was soft, it would stick with him throughout his life. When others said substantialness was good, he would retort that only empty rooms could hold things, and one had to empty old thoughts out of one's mind before acquiring new knowledge. Zhuang Zi, another Taoist thinker, liked to illustrate truths through vivid fables, using humorous language. Lao Zi and Zhuang Zi both believed that it was the common law of the universe that kept nature and society operating. Therefore, spirit and material, and human and nature could not be separated. Chinese tea culture, integrated with tea's natural and material functions and human spirit, absorbed the Taoist spirit. Therefore, while tea culture is mainly applied in a Confucian spirit, the formation of tea culture, acturally should mainly be attributed to the contribution made by the Taoist school.

The Combination of Human and Nature, and the World View of Tea Culture

According to the Taoist School, human and nature are unified. A person is a small world, and a cup of tea reflects the sea. Tea ceremony has assimilated this thought. Although tea is only a drink offered by nature, it contains natural law, and people should learn the law through drinking tea. Tea is the cream of nature, and people can learn about natural changes through brewing and drinking tea. Lu Yu regarded the process of making, brewing and drinking tea as an art reflecting natural beauty. When the ancients brewed tea, they ground tea cakes, or the newly picked and baked tea first, then sifted it through a fire sieve, and put the most even and tender powder into a boiler. It would change wonderfully when the water boiled, and the water and tea blended with each other. People could appreciate natural beauty through observing the change. Lu Yu vividly described the tea dust which was just put into the boiler "as floating date flowers in an annular pond," or "as the newly-grown green duckweed on a winding pond or islet." Lu Yu also described the foam, the cream of tea, vividly: they were "as white as snow cover." Tea connoisseurs regarded tea as the cleanest and most beautiful thing in nature, so people should integrate themselves with nature while drinking it. Lu Quan, a poet in the Tang Dynasty, known as the Tea Submaster, felt as if misty rain and cool breezes were spraying on him, and the whole world was incomparably bright and clear when he drank tea. When he drank seven cups of tea, he felt as graceful as a fairy. Su Shi, a great writer of the Song Dynasty, liked to row a small boat, draw water from the river, and brew tea in the rural outskirts of a town, or by the river bank. He believed that by doing so, he invited the bright moon and its silver flame into his jar. Chinese tea connoisseurs believed that people should not only demand from nature, they should also care for and understand it, and treat it kindly so that they could live quietly and happily. There is much profound Taoist philosophy in a cup of tea.

Taoist Tea Connoisseurs Drank Tea to Preserve their Health

Taoists, who were called immortals, paid great attention to

preserving their health. They believed that tea could ensure good health and a long life. The immortals deified the Taoist ideas, and called them Taoism. The main precept was to discard all desires and worries from one's mind; the best method of preserving one's health was by keeping one's body and mind extremely peaceful. There were several ways to cultivate vital energy to reach the ideal state:

1. using the deep breath in the pubic region to regulate one's passages through which vital energy circulated;

2. reposing one's thoughts in nature or a part of the body;

3. imagining the brilliance of sunshine, rain and dew, and stars sprinkling one, washing one clean, and getting rid of diseases;

4. eating health food.

Because tea could help adjust one's mind, keep one's head, improve digestion, and dredge the channels, it became essential to Taoists. Zhu Quan, a famous expert of tea culture of the Ming Dynasty, often drink tea while eating fruits and pine nuts when he cultivated himself in the mountains. The Taoist method was consistent with the science of channels and collaterals and the pharmacodynamics of traditional Chinese medicine. Taoists advocated adjusting one's mind and physiological functions through drinking tea, which was their special contribution to tea culture.

The Taoist Values and Characteristics of Tea Connoisseurs

Taoists had an active outlook on nature. They did not believe in God's will, and wanted to coexist with heaven and earth. They advocated natural Taoist rites, which meant complying with the law of nature and they also encouraged retirement from the world. The two concepts seem to contradict each other. However, the idea actually resisted the common views on wealth, women's looks, wine, undeserved reputation and benefits, and intrigues. Tea connoisseurs reflected Taoist thought in tea ceremony, and freed themselves from depression. Most of them disciplined themselves with ascetic practices, so the teaset was also called *kujiejun* in the Yuan and Ming dynasties to express their lofty ideals. This tradition has been followed to modern times. When China was invaded by foreign countries, many intellectuals would rather drink tea with steamed maize bread every day than become lackeys. It was precisely because of such lofty integrity that China was able to rise from sufferings time and again.

Lao Zi and Zhuang Zi, founders of the Taoist School, often spoke or acted contrary to common views intentionally. According to Lao Zi, people in the world could never find contentment in seeking pleasure; only he was indifferent to pleasure, for he had realized the hidden danger behind high positions and great wealth. Zhuang Zi expressed his views, which were also out of keeping with common ones, more vividly and clearly. According to him, wise men were admired because there were too many confused people in the world; if everyone became wise, there would be no wise man. Although the rhinoceros was a large animal, it could not catch a mouse. Chinese tea connoisseurs tried to learn the characters of Lao Zi and Zhuang Zi. For example, despite of the job's low social status, Lu Yu chose to became an actor; he refused to take a post in the court, and devoted himself to the study of tea culture. Zhu Quan, a famous tea connoisseur of the Ming Dynasty, who was a member of the imperial house, built a tomb for himself in a remote mountain in South China when he was still young so that he could devote himself to the study of the Taoist and Buddhist schools. It seemed to the tea connoisseurs that even beggars were better than corrupt officials, for beggars were pure in mind. Thus, Taoist tea culture was more suited to scholars and common people than the literati and officialdom. The tea art and tea ceremony of the former were natural and unrestrained.

The Status of Buddhism in Tea Culture

When talking of Chinese tea culture, attention is often paid to its relationship with Buddhism. There is a saying both in China and Japan that "tea and Chan is an integration." Although Chan is only a Buddhist sect, it has made a great contribution to the formation of the spirit of tea ceremony, and has played an important role in spreading tea culture throughout the East. The first disseminator of Japanese Buddhism was also the first tea master and the founder of the Japanese tea ceremony. The unique characteristics of Chinese Buddhist tea ceremony aroused great attention among Japanese monks.

Tea culture was closely related to earthly reality and society, while Buddhism stressed paradise. Chinese tea culture mainly stressed the love of life and optimism, while Buddhism emphasized bitterness and loneliness. The Chan sect solved the contradiction, and as a result, the two approaches were integrated.

China is a large smelting furnace, in which foreign thoughts have to be smelted before they take root in China. This is not because Chinese culture is "conservative" and "exclusive." In fact, China was quite open and magnanimous towards foreign culture in the early and medium stages of feudal society, especially during the Tang Dynasty when tea culture was created. Buddhism was spread from South Asia to China. At first, it was combined with the school of the emperor Huang and Lao Zi (a Taoist sect of the Warring States period and the early Han Dynasty. The emperor Huang and Lao Zi were honored as the founders of the Taoist school, hence the name). Taoists started to advocate tea drinking. However, it was during the Tang Dynasty that Buddhist thought and tea culture became fully integrated.

Most of the Buddhist sects that spread to China belonged to Great Vehicle, which developed from some Buddhist sects between the first and second century. Great Vehicle held that all living creatures could become Buddha, and equal stress should be laid on benefit to oneself and to others while practicing Buddhism. Buddhists regarded their doctrines as the best, hence the name "Great Vehicle,"; the sects advocating self-moksa (release from the cycle of rebirth) were deprecated as the "Little Vehicle". For example, the Sanlun, Sukhavati, Vinaya and Faxiang were all Great Vehicle sects which spread from India. However, these religious doctrines were not to the liking of the Chinese people. For example, according to the Sanlun sect, people should not be afraid of death, and should "cry for living." However, we Chinese people had such a deep love for life that we could not accept the idea that one could only become happy after one dies. According to the Sukhavati sect, the world was a dirty land, while we regarded land as our mother, on which there were beautiful grass and trees, and magnificent seas. How could we believe such beautiful land was dirty? Li Shimin, the first emperor of the Tang Dynasty, claimed to be a descendant of Lao Zi—Li Er. The emperor flew into a rage when a monk told him that his family name had nothing to do with that of Lao Zi. The emperor said that since the monk had told him the knife of Buddha could not hurt people, he would like to try it on him after he prayed to Buddha for seven days. The monk had no choice but to say that the emperor was Buddha, and he prayed to him for seven days. Thus he escaped death. It was clear that during the Tang Dynasty Buddhist reform had to be carried out so the Buddhist theories could be integrated with Chinese culture. Thus Tiantai, Huayan and some other sects, which were similar to Chinese culture and ideologies, came into being. However, only the Chan sect really turned into a Chinese Buddhist sect. It advocated practicing Buddhism by sitting in meditation in order to become peaceful in mind. It was similar to the Taoist practice of sitting in meditation and the Confucian views on one's inner accomplishment; it was beneficial to one's health, and enabled purification of one's mind to improve one's realm of spirit. Hui Neng (638-713), the sixth patriarch of the Chan sect in the prosperous period of the Tang Dynasty, advocated insight, expressed in the observation that "the butcher who lays down his knife at once becomes a Buddha." According to him, people could become Buddhists without becoming monks or nuns. Therefore, the court no longer needed to settle disputes over land between monasteries, and matters became convenient for the people.

With the appearance of the Chan sect, Buddhism started to have Chinese characteristics, and became consistent with tea culture. The Chan sect made contributions to promoting tea culture in the following three aspects:

1. Popularizing the practice of drinking tea.

According to the *Records of What Feng Saw and Heard* written by Feng Yan in the Tang Dynasty, "Southerners liked drinking tea, while northerners did not often drink tea at first. In the middle years of the Kaiyuan reign, the master of taming demons in the Divine Rock Temple on the Taishan Mountain developed the Chan sect energetically. The monks were neither allowed to sleep nor have supper while sitting in meditation at night, but they were allowed to drink tea. So each of them brewed tea and drank. People followed their example and tea-drinking thus became a custom.... Many tea shops were opened in the city, from which everyone could buy tea. Tea produced on the mountain was great in variety and amount, and was transported by boat and carriages from the Yangtze and Huai River valleys."

2. Developing tea plantation and planting tea on mountains.

It was expensive for monasteries to buy tea for monks, so the monks in some areas started to develop tea plantations or planted tea on mountains. Most of the monasteries were built in remote mountains, with excellent water and soil, and clean air, all of which were beneficial to tea plantation. Ji Gong, Lu Yu's master, planted tea by himself, and devoted himself to the study of tea. Many varieties of famous tea were produced by monasteries in the Tang Dynasty. The monks on Mount Putuo planted many tea trees, and "Putuo Buddhist tea" became famous. The tradition of tea plantation was retained until the Ming Dynasty. According to Li Rihua, who lived in the Ming Dynasty, an old monk of Mount Putuo presented him a small bag of White Crag tea as a gift. Its fresh smell gladdened his heart and refreshed his mind. Many monasteries were built in Jian'an in the Southern Tang Dynasty, and most of them planted excellent tea because both monks and pilgrims drank tea and monasteries possessed land. In addition, the monks had enough time to study the skills of planting, making, brewing and tasting tea. As a result, they promoted the development of tea culture, and Jian'an City became a famous tea production base   during the Song Dynasty.

3. Treating tea art with meditative mind, and creating the Buddhist realm of tea ceremony.

According to its philosophical views, the Chan sect stressed the tempering and remoulding of one's disposition to find one's true self. When a person's spirit reached the cleanest and most healthy state, he would understand truths. Tea could help him keep calm and clear-minded while sitting in meditation. Therefore, tea's distinguishing features were similar to those of Buddhism. The monks of the Chan sect drank tea not only to refresh themselves; they also connected the realm of tea with that of the Chan sect, and appreciated that the true essence of the world was to seek peace of mind. Jiao Ran, a famous monk of the Tang Dynasty, was a tea connoisseur and poet. He was a friend of Lu Yu, and they often studied tea ceremony and Buddhist doctrine, and wrote poems together. They also described their feelings about drinking tea, blending the fragrance of tea, natural and flowing verses, and profound Buddhist thoughts. According to Jiao Ran, after drinking a cup of tea, one would no longer feel in a daze, but feel as frank and open as heaven and earth. After drinking another cup of tea, one would feel as if the spirit was cleansed by gentle rain. According to the Chan sect, one could only become a Buddha after getting rid of infatuation—the largest obstacle—and tea could help achieve the purpose. After drinking the third cup of tea, a person would understand the nature of things. According to the Chan sect, it was impossible for people to get rid of their worries intentionally. They had to tranquilize their hearts to grasp the spirit of tea ceremony, which was to study the relationships between tea and mountains and rivers, nature, heaven and earth, and man, and between the human and the material, and body and mind.

Other sects, as well as the Chan sect, had their own theories of tea ceremony.

For example, tea culture flourished in Tibet's monasteries. Tibetans regarded tea as the wonder of enshrining and worshiping Buddha. Monasteries granted tea to common people as the blessing of God and Buddha. Hundred-year old brick tea has been kept in the Jokhang Temple in Lhasa till the present day. The Chinese people often said that "the older the wine, the better, while the newer the tea, the better." The 100-year-old tea is no longer useful as a drink, but the monks regard it as the monastery's protective shield. According to the description of a missionary of the Qing Dynasty, 4,000 lamas attended a large tea party held by the Karwenpalmo Lamasery, ordinary believers lay on the ground to worship Buddha, young monks held hot boilers and gave tea to the people, and people started to sing songs of praise. Because it was served as part of the Buddhist rites, tea became imbued with mystery. Buddha was to save all beings, so large boilers had to be used for such tea parties so that enough tea could be given to the people. The tea parties held by the Chan monasteries of Central Plains accentuated the adjustment of one's mind with tea to give full scope to one's ability to find one's true self, while the tea parties held by Tibetan monasteries regarded tea as a wonder granted by the gods in paradise. This view was more characteristic of objective idealism, and entirely different from the spirit of the tea ceremony of the Chan sect.

We have approached the spirit of the Chinese tea ceremony from the angles of the Confucian, Taoist and Buddhist schools. However, they are not isolated, but integrated with, and draw lessons from, each other. They have won support among the people in daily life. People can grasp many profound truths without going through the complicated forms of tea art. In the late Qing Dynasty and the early Republic of China (1912-1949) when China was in turmoil, and the people were destitute, scholars often put a brush pot, some books, and a simple tea set on their tables to express their elegant ideals. The common people often placed a teaset on a square table in the central room of their house, and the whole family would drink tea together at night. After thousands of years of extraction and purification, the spirit of the tea ceremony has penetrated deeply into the blood of the Chinese nation.

Chapter 5
Teahouse Culture

Teahouses, those public places in cities and towns where people gathered to drink tea, took shape during the Tang Dynasty, and flourished during the Song Dynasty. They were popular in South China, for southerners loved drinking tea, and they could also be found everywhere in North China. There were various types of teahouse. Many varieties of tea were served in teahouses, including ordinary tea, ginger tea with seasonings, peppermint tea and plum tea. In terms of their social function, the teahouses of the Tang and Song dynasties, however, only acted as meeting places for townspeople.

Considerable progress was made in the colorful teahouse culture from the Ming and Qing dynasties, when teahouse culture was integrated with regional culture.

Ba-Shu Culture and Sichuan Teahouses

Ba-Shu is one of China's earliest famous tea producing areas. The local people have kept up the hobby of drinking tea until the present. As the proverb goes, "there are few clear days, but many teahouses" in Sichuan Province, Chengdu City was most noted for its teahouses of various sizes. The large ones had hundreds of seats, while the small ones, only a few. Sichuan teahouses stressed good service, elegant styles of shop fronts, and excellent tea, teasets and operation skills. Traditional Sichuan teahouses served customers with red copper teapots, tin saucers, teacups with covers made of Jingdezhen porcelain, *tuocha*—a bowl-shaped compressed tea leaves— and tearoom keepers expert at all manner of work.

However, Sichuan teahouses not only attracted people's attention with their great number and excellent service, but also with their social functions.

Sichuan Province, a beautiful place, is rich in resources, and its local culture flourished in ancient times. During the Three Kingdoms Period, Zhuge Liang helped Liu Bei establish the State of Shu in Sichuan, which played an important role in the development of Ba-Shu culture, and Sichuanese preserved the tradition of concerning themselves with state affairs. Because Sichuan was difficult of access, it was hard for local people to get information about state affairs. The Sichuan teahouses played an important role in spreading this information. The local people went to teahouses not only to drink tea, but also to exchange information. The most important function of the teahouses was that people could chat with each other there. Each large teahouse was a society in microcosm. Teahouses couild be found everywhere in Chongqing, Chengdu, and other large and small cities and towns throughout Sichuan Province. In the old days, many Chongqing people liked to linger in teahouses. They would go there immediately after they got up, and some of them even washed their faces there. They would drink tea and have breakfast, and then chat with each other. Though simply furnished, Sichuan teahouses were elegant yet informal, making people feel at home. Customers could sit at tables or lie on bamboo deck chairs while drinking tea. Whenever a customer entered a teahouse, and lay on a deck chair, the waiter would greet him warmly, and make tea for him. The tearoom keeper would take off the cover of the teacup with his left hand, while making tea with the right hand. His two hands worked very well together, and dozens of cups would be filled with tea in an instant without a single drop being spilled. The manoeuvre reflected the tradition of "even cream" in the tea culture, and also demonstrated beautiful rhythm and superb skill. Sichuanese liked drinking *tuocha*, the bowl-shaped compressed mass of tea leaves with a strong taste and delicate fragrance, especially when they talked for a long time, as *toucha's* qualities were very long-lasting. Some people would drink from early morning till noon, and ask the tearoom keeper to keep their teacups so that they could continue to drink after lunch. Quick-witted, and skilled in debates, the Sichuanese could talk with old or new friends about everything in an accomplished way. Sichuan teahouses served as information exchange centers, which was their most important function.

They also served as unofficial courts. Local people would gather at a teahouse, and ask the powerful security group heads, rural elites or the *Paoge* Master (a secret society in the provinces in the southwest part of China in the old days, or its member) to settle a dispute. God knew whether the resolution was fair or not. However, the practice showed that Sichuanese regarded teahouses as fair places to settle disputes. Compared with teahouses elsewhere, Sichuan teahouses had more obvious political and social functions.

It was not true that Sichuan teahouses were always vulgar, for many scholars often went there. It is said that some Sichuan authors liked to write in teahouses, for they could "keep quiet in a noisy neighborhood," and draw their inspiration from teahouses. On fair days, the seats of a local teahouse would be placed outside so that people could appreciate Sichuan opera, *qingyin* (a type of ballad-singing popular in Sichuan Province), *shuochang* (a genre of popular entertainment mainly including talking and singing), and puppet shows. The teahouses served as public places for holding folk cultural activities.

Sichuan teahouses also served as economic exchanges, an important function which was often ignored. Special teahouses for businessmen in Chengdu City were installed with comfortable seats, where tea was served with light refreshments, and people could order dishes at any time. They were very convenient for people to negotiate business. In the old days, people also purchased official positions and sought higher rank in teahouses. Businessmen also often gathered at village teahouses.

With their political, economic and cultural functions, Sichuan teahouses played an important role in making good the omissions and deficiencies of society. Though they were not learned and refined places, tea's cultural and social functions were fully reflected in the teahouses.

Wu-Yue Culture and Hangzhou Teahouses

Situated a the remote area far from the national political center, the lower Yangtze River valley retained the cultural features that formed the unique style and characteristics of the ancient culture of the states of Wu and Yue (hereinafter referred to as Wu-Yue Culture). The area was long inhabited by the ancient tribes in the east. It is one of China's famous tea-producing areas and the birthplace of Chinese tea culture, for green tea produced in Zhejiang Province played a decisive role. Several important factors contributed to the region's significance for tea culture.

Noted for its beautiful landscape, the area has not only suitable natural conditions for producing tea, but also the artistic environment for tasting tea. It is rich in famous teas, mountains and rivers. Chinese tea culture always advocates natural agreement. Therefore, Wu-Yue Area, including Taihu Lake and the Qiantangjiang River valleys became a large natural "teahouse."

Southeastern China is a Buddhist and Taoist center. However, because people there respect ancient customs and local traditions, Buddhism has kept fewer of its original features in the area than in Qinghai, Tibet and other western regions. Any culture has to be remoulded to suit local customs. Esoteric Buddhism is practiced most in the Qinghai-Tibet area, which has retained the original features of Indian Buddhism; in Beijing, the Vinaya school has been remoulded to suit Chinese culture; in the Wu-Yue area, Zen practiced. It is a completely remoulded Buddhist school which is closer to Taoist and Confucian thought—China's "original" culture. Therefore, the famous Wu-Yue tea producing region integrates Confucian, Taoist and Buddhist thought, a combination which created the system of Chinese tea culture.

The economy of the lower Yangtze River valley has flourished since the Sui and Tang dynasties. The Southern Song government had its capital in Lin'an, and as a result, the local culture developed rapidly. The area is greatly affected by the fresh cultural flavor of regions south of the Yangtze, and the local culture is also blended with ancient customs. The ancient Chinese tea culture has changed dramatically in modern times, but its essence has been retained secretly not only in the Wu-Yue area, but also in Fujian and Guangdong provinces. Up to now tea markets in Zhejiang Province have been the most flourishing, and various organizations has been established. These include the Lu Yu and Jiao Ran tea groups, folk tea parties in Huzhou City; the modernized China Tea Research Institute and the tea museum covering past and present tea lore in Hangzhou;   the teahouses by West Lake, and the Tea Connoisseurs Association, a combination of teachouse, tea party and tea research institute.

Hangzhou teahouse culture originated in the Southern Song Dynasty (1127-1279). After the Jin people (an ethnic minority in North China which established the Jin Dynasty during 1115-1234) overthrew the Northern Song Dynasty (960-1127), the Southern Song Dynasty established its capital in Hangzhou. The Confucian studies and palace culture of the Central Plains spread to the city, where tea markets and teahouses prospered. A book records that "Hangzhou teahouses keep up their appearances with seasonal flowers and famous paintings, sell excellent tea, soup and wine throughout the year, for instance, seven-treasure *leicha* tea, fried dough twists, onion or *yangutang* tea in winter, and *meihua* (plum blossom) wine in summer." Thus we can see that the custom of combining paintings and calligraphy in Hangzhou teahouses and various popular drinking methods were developed as far back as the Southern Song Dynasty. *Leicha* tea, a health drink made of pounded tea, sesame, rice flowers and other food, could work up an appetite. The *Yangutang* tea referred to might be *yandou* tea now popular in Zhejiang Province. It was a common practice to add onions and gingers to tea during the Song Dynasty.

The present teahouses in the Wu-Yue Area are fewer than those in Sichuan Province because most of the Zhejiang people drink tea at home. However, the cultural atmosphere of Hangzhou tearooms is much stronger.

The Hangzhou teahouses have several features. They emphasize making tea with famous water, and tasting it in an excellent environment, thus achieving the true objective of tea art.

Unlike Sichuan teahouses, which have tea seats, complete teasets and skillful tearoom attendants, Hangzhou tearooms are valued in their genuineness. *Longjing* tea is regarded as the best tea in Hangzhou. The best-quality *longjing* tea is hard to come by, for it does not originate in Longjing Village, but from Lion Peak. However, people can taste the superfine or first-grade *longjing* tea. It is classified as green tea, which keeps tea's natural color. A cup of *longjing* tea is a work of art with its clear tea water, beautiful leafbuds, and mild and sweet taste similar to that of sweet dew.

Good quality water is of vital importance to it. Water from the Running Tiger Spring is regarded as the best; the water quality in other areas, while inferior, is still much better than those of inland waters. People enjoy themselves visiting the West Lake and Temple of Inspired Seclusion, and drinking first-grade *longjing* tea with water from the Running Spring. The charm lies in the fact that both tea and water keep their original color, fragrance, taste and natural qualities when people drink in pavilions, terraces and open halls, or in mountain valleys.

Tearooms by the West Lake are full of celestial, Buddhist and learned and refined atmosphere.

In Hangzhou, most tearooms are elegant, simple and unsophisticated. Few are like the teahouses in Beijing and Tianjin, which combine *shuochang* (a genre of popular entertainment including mainly talking and singing) and *quyi* (Chinese folk art forms). None is like the Shanghai *fuchaguan* (teahouses which also serve as public baths). Few adopt the practice of drinking tea with refreshments and meat gruel comon in Guangzhou and Hong Kong teahouses. Scholars' reading rooms and Buddhist meditation rooms are both called rooms. Thus Hangzhou teahouses are called tearooms because of their elegant, quiet and beautiful artistic conception. Small shops attached to the tearooms sell handiworks such as Hangzhou fans, bamboo carvings, small images of Ji Gong, or West Lake lotus root starch.

People feel that the lake and sky, and they themselves and the tea are at one when they drink tea in the tearooms along the Su and Bai causeways; when they appreciate the gurgling Running Tiger Spring and its folk stories, they can sense the wonderful Taoist celestial atmosphere. When they drink *longjing* tea while listening to the gurgling spring and the clear and melodious sound of bells, watching the wreaths of incense smoke and the devoted Buddhists chanting in the Temple of Inspired Seclusion, visitors will realize the truth of Buddhist allegorical words or gestures even if they themselves are not Buddhists. Decorated with paintings, calligraphy and poetic prose works, the Association of Tea Connoisseurs beside the Xileng Printing Office has a learned and refined style. Thus people can feel tea's cultural flavor in Hangzhou tearooms not only because of the methods of brewing and making tea, but also because of the historic atmosphere. Tea is full of celestial airs, for it is produced in the area where the remains of holy hermits and immortals lie.

The beautiful scenery of Hangzhou City provides an excellent natural environment for the development of the tearooms by the West Lake.

The whole Hangzhou City is a large natural "teahouse." Tea integrates naturally with man, heaven and earth, mountains and rivers, cloud and mists, bamboo and stones, and flowers and trees. Humanity and nature, and tea culture and Wu-Yue culture also become melded. Local teahouses also have the function of settling civil disputes. When both sides agree, they may go to a teahouse to settle the dispute in public. Though opposing each other, the two sides have to speak in a mild tone when defending themselves in an elegant teahouse. The losing side will have to pay for tea, which is called *chipincha*. As a result, the parties are able to distinguish clearly between right and wrong without hurting each other, and manifest the golden mean principle and the theory of governing by doing nothing that is against nature.

Tianjin Teahouses, Shanghai *Fuchaguan* Teahouses and Guangdong Tearooms

Tianjin became a city after the Jin and Yuan dynasties to service the Great Canal. It has been an important industrial and commercial metropolis in North China in the modern times. Because it is close to Beijing, the capital, Tianjin teahouses imitated those in Beijing to meet the needs of industrial and commercial development, as well as those of ordinary people. In old China, besides formal teahouses, the public places for tea-drinking included public baths, brothels, restaurants and tea stalls.

As in the large Beijing teahouses, the formal Tianjin teahouses sold refreshments, accompanied by the singing of opera arias, storytelling and *dagu* (a versified story sung to the accompaniment of a small drum and other instruments). Every customer was served with a teapot and cup, while groups of customers were provided with a teapot and several cups. People of various trades drank tea while eating refreshments and appreciating performances. Some of them came to teahouses to look for jobs, such as lacquering, bricklaying and woodwork. Teahouses were often antique trading floors. In the *Sandexuan* Teahouse, craftsmen drank tea and looked for jobs in the morning, while at noon, storytelling and *dagu* were performed; in the *Donglaixuan* Teahouse, cooks sang opera arias in the morning, while in the evening, actors/actress and amateur performers sang together. Some famous Beijing opera performers often went to the *Donglaixuan* Teahouse. People from all walks of life killed time, read newspapers, exchanged information or played chess in the teahouses. Unlike Beijing teahouses, which were carefully classified, Sichuan teahouses or Hangzhou tearooms, which have their unique local features, most of the Tianjin teahouses met the needs of business people from different parts of China.

In the old days, customers in Tianjin restaurants would be greeted with a cup of top-grade tea as soon as they arrived so that they could refresh themselves and whet their appetite. After that, formal courses would be served. Tea would be served again after the meal so that customers could rest for a while before leaving. It was a good tradition. In such a way, Tianjin teahouses gave full play to the social and economic development of the city. The old local residents drank tea three times a day. The cultural atmosphere of the teahouses, however, was not strong, which was a common characteristic of the teahouses in North China.

However, the teahouses in Shanghai, another modern industrial and commercial metropolis, had a stronger cultural atmosphere. In the past, the tearooms in gardens were often filled with guests and friends. Many sons and daughters of the rich went to tearooms to learn civilized manners and mingle with men of letters and scholars and to pose as lovers of culture. Although, compared with Beijing teahouses where tea was served without refreshments, Shanghai tearooms had a less literary atmosphere, they could be regarded as learned and refined places in Shanghai. The most typical teahouse with local features was situated in the old Chenghuangmiao (Temple of Town God) area. For example, in the old *Deyilou* Teahouse, the customers on the ground floor were small tradesmen, porters and other laborers, and the stalls at the gate sold sesame seed cakes. The second floor, where customers drank tea while listening to storytelling, had a greater cultural atmosphere, and the third floor, where bird connoisseurs gathered, was full of the joy of life. The most quietly and tastefully laid out tearoom was situated in *Yuyuan* Garden, neighboring *Chenghuangmiao*. Though inferior to Suzhou gardens, the traditional zigzag southern private garden was very beautiful. The tearooms close to ponds and bamboos were very elegant. Shanghai people called teahouses *fuchaguan* to express their longing for leisure. We can thus see that teahouses were popular in modern cities.

The teahouses in Guangzhou, another modern city, looked grander. The local people called breakfast *zaocha* (morning-tea). If a Cantonese said "I would like to invite you to drink tea tomorrow," he meant to invite you for a meal. The old Guangdong tearooms were inexpensive. Regular customers would be served with a cup of tea, and two steamed buns stuffed with diced grilled pork, steamed dumplings with the dough gathered at the top, or dumplings with shrimp stuffing. However, present teahouses are different. A waitress serves customers with a pot of strong tea as soon as they arrive, and asks them to select from a great variety of refreshments on the food cart.

Some small village teahouses in Guangdong were like little and dainty waterside pavilions with bamboo or bark fences. Customers were served with a cup of tea with thick stalks and large leaves, and two steamed dumplings with the dough gathered at the top or other refreshments, but compared with the teahouses in Guangzhou and Hongkong, they had a stronger cultural and artistic ambience. Though not as learned and refined as the tearooms by the West Lake, the simple and unadorned teahouses were full of the appeal of waterside villages. The villagers drank tea three times a day in the waterside teahouses. In the morning, they appreciated the rising sun and misty morn; at noon, the passing boats setting sails or sculling; in the evening, the moon rising in the east, which was reflected in the water. As a result, their weariness dissolved. The waterside teahouses in Guangdong were called tancha. Tan meant to enjoy. People could learn tea's taste, and the joys and sorrows of life. Compared with the teahouses in large cities, they were rich in the philosophies of life and nature.

Beijing Teahouse Culture

Beijing teahouses epitomized the advantages of other local teahouses, and were noted for their great variety, complete functions, and rich and profound cultural aims.

Historically, there were many kinds of Beijing teahouses, including *dachaguan* (great teahouses), *qingchaguan* (teahouses serving tea without refreshments), *shuchaguan* (teahouses where storytelling was performed), *erhunpu* (teahouses selling both tea and wine and dinners, *hongluguan* (teahouses installed with red stoves) and *yechaguan* (teahouses in the country). There were also innumerable tea stalls and booths. The teahouses became the meeting place for people of all sorts. It was more convenient for people to carry out activities in teahouses than in formal hall or restaurants, for it cost less money, and one felt more at ease meeting friends in a teahouse than at home. Strangers without families could also relax in teahouses. Teahouses became popular because of the special composition of the population. Therefore, teahouses of various forms and with varied functions spread all over Beijing. I would like to introduce several varieties from the angle of their cultural and social functions.

Storytelling and folk literature in *shuchaguan*

Novels of the Ming and Qing dynasties occupy an important place in the history of Chinese literature. However, unlike Western classical fiction, ancient Chinese novels, especially full-length masterpieces, were not written solely in the writers' studies, but were revised according to story-tellers' scripts. They became the oral literature of the performers in teahouses or restaurants. Such masterpieces included The Romance of Three Kingdoms and Outlaws of the Marsh. Because ancient Chinese novels took root among the masses, they displayed a greater vitality than other literary works. Teahouse culture since the Song and Yuan dynasties made a special contribution to the development of the novel, and Beijing *shuchaguan* was the best evidence of the method of development.

In the old days, there were many *shuchaguan* in Beijing, where tea only acted as a medium, and people came there mainly to listen to storytelling. Storytelling was performed two times a day: from 3:00pm to 6:00pm or 7:00pm, and from 7:00pm or 8:00pm to 11:00pm or 12:00pm. Sometimes the storytelling started one or two hours earlier, providing opportunities for ordinary performers to practice. Before the performance started, tea was served without refreshments so that passers-by could have a break and quench their thirst. After the storytelling began, the teahouses only received customers who listened to it. Customers would refresh themselves with tea while listening. They included all sorts of people, such as unlucky officials, politicians and office workers, shop managers and accountants, old ladies enjoying themselves, and the toiling masses. The bill was called payment for storytelling instead of payment for tea because customers went to the teahouses to listen to storytelling, while tea only acted as a supplement. Famous *shuchaguan* were exquisitely furnished with cane or wooden tables and chairs, and decorated with works of calligraphy and paintings to build an atmosphere for storytelling. A teahouse would invite a storyteller to perform well in advance. A long story would last two or three months. The teahouse took 30 percent of the income, while the storyteller received 70 percent. As an intellectual, the storyteller was greatly respected by the teahouse manager. There were all kinds of stories, including historical stories, such as *The Romances of Three Kingdoms*, *Records of the Eastern* and *Western Han Dynasties*, and *Romance of Sui* and *Tang Dynasties*; tales of *complicated legal cases, such as the Cases Handled by Lord Bao*, and *Cases Handled by Lord Peng*; and stories about gods and spirits, such as *The Journey to the West*, *The Biography of Lord Ji*, and *The Romance of the Canonized Gods*. *The Strange Tales from the Make Do Studio*, which was full of beautiful love stories, had to be told in a way which suited both refined and popular taste, for if told in popular terms, its original intention was lost, while if recounted in refined terms, it was difficult to understand.

Customers enjoyed themselves listening to the interesting stories about gods and spirits told by excellent story-tellers, who expanded the meanings of the stories to illustrate the fickleness of the world.

Various *quyi* (Chinese folk art forms) were performed in the *shuchaguan* in the Tianqiao area; they included *meihua dagu, lihua dagu,* and storytelling in Beijing and Tangshan dialects with drum accompaniment. The stories were either taken from voluminous storytelling books or newly-compiled in order to be fashionable and to suit the contemporary environment.

People drank tea in *shuchaguan* to increase their historical knowledge, kill time and amuse themselves. So *shuchaguan* were best suited to old people. I remembered that during the initial post-liberation period, my grandmother's old neighbor, who pulled a pedicab, used to take her to a teahouse in Gulou. After she listened to storytelling for several hours, the neighbor would pick her up and return her in the evening. Our family would invite him to have supper at home. At present, there are increasing problems of the aged. A revival of the *Shuchaguan* would be a nice place for today's old people.

Entertainment in Beijing's *qingchaguan* and *qichaguan* (teahouses in which people played chess):

Though *shuchaguan* had a strong atmosphere of folk culture, they were monotonous. There were many *qingchaguan* in Beijing, providing places for people from all walks of life to entertain themselves elegantly. Tea was served without refreshments in these teahouses. Most of them were simply furnished with elegant square tables and wooden chairs, and teacups with covers were used. In spring, summer and autumn, a shelter would be set outside or in the courtyard of the teahouse. The seats in the front shelter were for ordinary customers, while those in the room were for regular customers. Comfortable seats were set in the courtyard. Wooden signboards with characters such as *maojian, yuqian, queshe,* and *dafang* were hung in front of the gate or under the roof of the shelter to show that the teahouse was selling first-class tea. The teahouses opened at five every morning. Most of the customers were idlers, including the old and young survivors of the late Qing Dynasty, children of families in decline, and common people. Residents of old Peking were accustomed to getting up early to do exercises, which were called *liuzao*. They would go for a walk in quiet places with their birds in cages, then do exercises by reed ▬▬▬▬▬ n the banks of the moat. When they and the birds breathed enough fresh air, they would return to the town and enter teahouses. They would hang the birdcages on a pole and drink tea while appreciating the birds' calls. The trained larks, babblers, *hongdian, landian* and other species could call in more than 10 ways, and imitate the cries gpies, titmice, hawks, cuckoos, wild geese and babies. The old customers then talked about their experiences of cultivating tea and keeping pets, engaged in small talk, or commented on current events. They developed a unique method of integrating tea and nature. The shopkeepers of *qingchaguan* helped well-known pet keepers to organize *chaniaohui* (parties to appreciate both tea and birds) to solicit customers. They would send invitation cards on fancy stationery and red envelopes to old customers, and put up posters on the street. The pet keepers would go to the parties and old customers took pleasure in them, while teahouses could reap great profit. In winter, besides warming themselves and chatting in teahouses, customers liked to appreciate butterflies spreading their wings, and watch cricketfights, activities which added vitality to the bleak winter, and made their life more colorful. It was an unique scene in Beijing. In the afternoon, these old customers were replaced by businessmen or pedlars, who negotiated business at teahouses.

There were also *qichaguan* in Beijing where customers played chess. *Qichaguan* were simply furnished with timber or lumps of wood painted with chessboards, which were partly buried in the ground, or chessboards with benches on both sides. More than 10 customers would drink tea in a *qichaguan* while playing chess each afternoon. People of Beijing in old times, even the poor, had refined hobbies. *Qichaguan* was an example. When they played chess while drinking scented tea or other ordinary tea, the chessboard was like an battlefield of life, and they would temporarily forget about their sufferings. Because of this quality, tea was also called *wangyoujun* (Mr. Worry-free).

People went to *Yechaguan* (teahouses in the country) and seasonal tea sheds for outings to appreciate beautiful gardens. People of Beijing in old times loved going for outings. They went out to enjoy the beautiful scenery in spring, in summer to appreciate the lotus flowers, in autumn the maple leaves and in winter the Western Hills shimmering with snow. Some old people loved the melon sheds, bean poles, vineyards and fishponds on the outskirts of the city, so *yechaguan* appeared in these beautiful areas. For example, the *Maizi* Teashop at Chaoyangmenwai was established in a peaceful and secluded place surrounded by reeds and many ponds. Skillful fish farmers often went there to net water fleas. When the sun was sinking in the west, old men walked on crisscross footpaths between the fields, and gathered at the teahouse. The teahouse at Liupukang was surrounded by melon sheds and bean poles. Customers could appreciate rustic sights such as the flowers of cucumbers and eggplants, and butterflies while drinking tea, just as Lu Fangweng (Lu You) had taken great pleasure in chatting about the cultivation of mulberries and hemps with old farmers. People recovered their original simplicity in such an environment. The Vineyard Teahouse at Chaoyangmenwai was close to a clear stream in the west, ling and tea ponds to the east and south and many grape trellises and towering old trees surrounded by low fences to the north. Scholars often went there to play chess, solve riddles or write poems.

Good-quality water was rare in Beijing, and most of the city water was bitter. The Qing Palaces took water from the sweet and refreshing spring at the Jade Spring Hill in the northwest part of Beijing. Because of the poor quality city water it was best to build *yechaguan* in beautiful places near excellent springs. The *Shanglong* and *Xialong* teahouses at Andingmenwai were such teahouses. They were only about 100 paces apart. The Prosperity Temple was situated there in the Qing Dynasty, and there was a dozen *mu* of pond to the north. When the 300-year-old "memorial tree to King Wen" blossomed, the fragrance spread all over the courtyard. There was also a well with sweet, refreshing and clear water outside the temple. Rich with cultural relics, beautiful views and excellent water, it was an excellent place to drink tea. The shopkeeper built a canopy near the well to sell tea, wine and steamed buns. The teahouse was a small earthen structure standing on the slope. When customers drank tea with the water from the *Shanglong* Well while looking out the windows at the old trees in the courtyard and near the well, at the reeds and lings in the pond, and the sun dipping to the Western Hills, and while listening to the bells from the old temple, the roosters crowing and the dogs barking in the village, they could feel the sweetness and bitterness of life. The teahouses by the Gaoliangqiao and Baishiqiao bridges flourished because pleasure-boats passed there during the Qing Dynasty. *Yechaguan*, quiet spots away from the noisy city, enlivened the people's life and added natural interest to tea-drinking. Although not as secluded and quiet as the teahouses by the West Lake in Hangzhou City, they were simple and unadorned and, thus, closer to the true spiritual qualities of the Chinese tea ceremony.

Such teahouses also included seasonal tea sheds in parks. The most famous ones were situated at Little Western Heaven by the North Lake, in which lotuses grew. Almond tea, mashed peas and *suzao* meat were also served.

People had social contacts in *Dachaguan* (great teahouses) with catering services. The old Beijing *dachaguan* had various functions. They served tea and food, and provided excellent service to people in various trades, such as businessmen and scholars. *Teahouse*, the famous opera written by Lao She, described the model of the old Beijing *dachaguan*. The *Lao She Teahouse* at Qianmen has carried on the tradition and opened a way for those who follow. *Dachaguan* became popular because of their multiple functions and good service.

Tianhuixuan Teahouse at Dianmenwai was the most famous old Beijing *dachaguan*; *Huifengxuan* Teahouse at Donganmenwai was second only to it.

The teahouses were tastefully furnished. The first counter at the entrance was in charge of take-outs and the accounts for the front hall, the second counter, for the accounts of the *yaoshuan* or middle hall connecting the front and back halls, and the back counter, the back hall and comfortable seats. Each counter received different types of customer. In some *dachaguan*, the back and middle halls were connected with each other while, in some, the halls were separated by a courtyard.

The teahouses served customers with exquisite teasets. Teacups with covers kept the tea sanitary and warm. Pekinese stressed etiquette while drinking tea. They used the covers of teacups to stir tea and cover their mouths. Waiters would take good care of customers' teasets and seats so that they could continue to drink after lunch.

In terms of service, Beijing *dachaguan* also included *hongluguan* (teahouses installed with red stoves), *wowoguan* (teahouses serving tea with refreshments), and *banhuguan* (teahouses installed with a large copper pot).

Hongluguan were installed with red stoves which baked Manchurian and Chinese pastries. They served all kinds of pastries, which were smaller and more exquisite than those made by pastry shops. Customers could drink tea while sampling these pastries.

Wowoguan served various refreshments, including *aiwowo*, steamed sponge cakes, *paicha*, *pengao* and sesame seed cakes.

Characterized by a large copper pot, *banhuguan* suited both refined and popular taste.

Erhunpu served tea without refreshments, but provided dining and wining facilities. It supplied customers food cooked from raw materials provided by itself or brought by customers. For example, educational circles used to gather at the *Longhaixuan* Teahouse on Changanjie Street. During the late Qing Dynasty, new-type schools appeared suddenly in Baoding, and disputes often occurred between the Beijing and Baoding types. On such occasions, adherents of the Beijing type would hold a principal joint meeting at the teahouse to discuss countermeasures. This custom led to the Beijing type of education being sometimes called Longhai Type.

Dachaguan had many functions—people could drink tea, dine, make social contact, and entertain themselves there. They were broader in scope, and had a more profound influence than other teahouses. *Lao She Teahouse* is still popular among people from all walks of life today. Tea acted as a medium of contact and had great social functions in the *dachaguan*.

Chapter 6
Tea and Literature and Art

Representative Works of Tea Paintings

Chinese tea culture came into being at the height of the Tang Dynasty, and Chinese tea paintings began to appear at about the same time. However, tea paintings of this time, like other drinking banquet paintings or recreation paintings, just displayed tea drinking and did not form art works showing the special essence of tea. In *The Book of Tea* by Lu Yu, there were tea paintings, but they mainly displayed the process of brewing tea so that people could know more about tea. In a sense, they were simply like advertisements of new food. But many poets and calligraphers among tea drinkers, headed by Lu Yu, made many beautifully conceived poems in tea parties. This aroused later generations to associate between art and tea and made later painters and calligraphers meditate on art works more deeply.

Xiao Yi Wrangles Over the Masterpiece of Calligraphy Lan Ting by Strategy by Yan Liben in the Tang Dynasty is the earliest tea painting in the world. It shows one Confucianist and two monks drinking tea together. On the right, the monks and Confucianist are talking about Buddhism and Confucianism as they wait for the tea. On the left, two servants, one old and the other young, are brewing tea single-mindedly. The old servant is putting the teapot on the stove and brewing tea elaborately, while the young one is holding a bowl, waiting to present the brewed tea to his master. With the expressions of the characters being true to life, the painting is meticulously drawn, reflecting the simple way that the lower-level Confucianists and monks drank tea. It set a good precedent in it that tea painting should not only display the material life of tea brewing and drinking, but should mainly express some thought. The painting is pregnant with the meaning that the Confucianist and Buddhists talked about doctrine as they drank tea. It shows that talking about tea was more important than brewing tea.

The painting *Auspiciousness and Happiness* by Zhang Xuan displayed Emperor Minghuang of the Tang Dynasty drinking tea. In the painting, the emperor lies on his bed, with three maids of honor standing beside it. Another maid of honor is holding a teaset containing tea and fruit, and it appears that the emperor has just finished drinking tea and has ordered her to clear away the teaset. Judging from the teasets, some specialists in tea think that this painting shows the way of making tea with loose tea in the early Tang Dynasty. But culturally, we pay more attention to the two words "Auspiciousness and Happiness," which was what the painter tried to express. The anonymous painting, *Palace Music*, shows the grand scene of imperial ladies drinking tea. In the palace is a luxury table, displaying liquor, a large utensil holding the tea, and a ladle to scoop out the tea. The maids of honor are all holding musical instruments, their foreheads broad and their jaws wide, their clothes beautiful, and their buns high. They sit on refined embroidered seats, some holding a bowl with both hands and drinking tea, others playing the four-stringed Chinese lute, Xiao (a vertical bamboo flute) or other ancient musical instruments. Some maids of honor are standing in attendance, while a cat is lying under the table. It can be seen from the viewpoint of tea culture that tea and liquor did not interfere with each other, but the main content of the painting is the combination of tea with recreation.

Other tea paintings of the Tang Dynasty, according to documents, include the painting *Brewing Tea* and the painting *Figures of Ladies Brewing Tea*, but unfortunately they have been lost.

Overall, during the Tang Dynasty, which was the pioneering stage of tea paintings, painters depicted the details and scenes of tea brewing and drinking concretely and minutely, but they did not show the spiritual connotation of tea in any depth. After all, this opened up a new field for tea culture. By visible artistic means, people not only realized the effects of tea, but also began to heed its spiritual experience.

From the Five Dynasties to the Song Dynasty, tea paintings were rich in content. They displayed either large tea banquets of palaces and officialdom, or scholars drinking tea in their studies, or the common people appraising and drinking tea. As most were painted by famous painters, the artistry of tea painting was further raised. Among them are many rare works of a high order, and more than ten of them are used for textual research.

The painting *Han Xizai Attending an Evening Banquet*, painted by Gu Hongzhong during the Five Dynasties, depicts a large tea banquet. In it there are many vivid figures, who are drinking as women are dancing. Two maidservants are holding plates, on which the utensils look much like those in the painting *Auspiciousness and Happiness*. Therefore, some people think that at the banquet people drank both tea and liquor.

Zhao Ji, Emperor Huizong of the Northern Song Dynasty, though not good at ruling his state, was a rare artist. He had a good knowledge of chess, calligraphy, paintings, and *qin* (a seven-stringed plucked instrument in some ways similar to the zither). He specially liked tea art. His painting *Scholars' Gathering* is universally thought to depict a tea banquet. In a noble garden with a pool, mountain stones and willows, there is a big square table, on which are fruit, refreshments, and tea. Around the table are more than ten scholars. At the lower corner on the left some servants are brewing tea, with teasets, the stove, and the big basket for storing teasets for future use, clear and recognizable. Behind the tea table, between flowers and trees, is another table, on which there are an incense burner and a *qin*. This showed that scholars had made tea drinking elegant, not excluding music on the lute and the fragrance of flowers.

In terms of achievements in art, the tea paintings by Liu Songnian in the Southern Song Dynasty take the first place. His paintings handed down to us include *Rumpling Tea* (showing the tea art of the Song Dynasty), *Gambling Market in the Tea Plantation,* and *Lu Tong Brewing Tea.* The last two paintings, in particular, have both profound implications and are great achievements in art, setting an example to later generations.

The painting *Gambling Market in the Tea Plantation* depicts the appraisal of tea among common people. In it all the people, old and young, including women and children, have vivid expressions. The scene of appraisal of tea in a tea producing area is full of life. On the left a woman with a child is selling tea in her basket; in the middle a pedlar, with two baskets of tea on his shoulder pole, is also selling tea; on the right gamblers are appraising tea, which is the main theme of the painting. On either basket containing tea and teasets on an old man's shoulder pole is a tag, on which is written, "First-Class River Tea." Old men, women and children all focus their attention on those appraising tea on the right, a detail which makes the theme "appraising tea" more prominent. The people appraising tea all have teasets. They match each other for good tea, showing great concern for the result. This painting shows the appraisal of tea among common people in the Song Dynasty. Vivid, detailed, and true to life, it is both a masterpiece of art and a precious reference material for the study of the history of tea drinking.

The painting *Lu Tong Brewing Tea,* another tea painting by Liu Songnian, is vividly painted according to a poem on drinking tea written by Lu Tong, a poet during the Tang Dynasty. The painting depicts some scholars, who are drinking tea under the moon by mountain stones and bamboo bushes in the field. It mainly reflects the experience and happiness of people drinking tea. It deserves to be particularly noted, for it is a portrayal of tea art which approaches nature.

It can be seen from the tea paintings by Liu Songnian that in the Southern Song Dynasty tea culture influenced all walks of life and further increased its social effects.

In the Song Dynasty there were other paintings reflecting scholars drinking tea in their studies. For example, in the anonymous painting *Characters,* a scholar sits up straight in his study, where *qin,* books and paintings are placed on the desk, flowers are arranged in the middle, and a stove is put on the right. With the charcoal fire roaring, a child servant is working on the boiling tea. It is truly a leisurely and elegant scene.

The painting *Children Playing in Spring* by Su Hanchen of the Song Dynasty, shows many children tuning the *qin,* practicing calligraphy, playing games, and tasting tea. It has the rich flavor of life and implies the children's friendship.

In all, the Song Dynasty ushered in an epoch of tea paintings of great achievement.

In the Ming and Yuan dynasties, tea culture had two characteristics. One was that it had deeper philosophic thinking, advocating agreement with nature and blending with mountains and waters, heaven and earth, and the cosmos. The other was that tea drinking among common people was developed, and that the friendship and harmony of tea drinkers deeply influenced all manner of people. Excellent tea paintings in the Yuan and Ming dynasties also reflected these two aspects. However, in contrast, painters at that time paid more attention to the connotation of tea paintings than to techniques of tea culture. This conforms with the overall trend in the development of Chinese tea culture. After the Yuan and Ming dynasties, the Chinese feudal culture became mature, and social and ideological conflicts became sharper, making tea paintings at that time more profound.

Zhao Mengfu, a famous painter in the Yuan Dynasty, painted the painting *Appraising Tea* after the painting *Gambling Market in the Tea Plantation* by Liu Songnian in the Song Dynasty. The former attached more importance to the theme of appraising tea, deleted other figures, and displayed the psychology of the four central figures in the latter by painting them in minute detail. In the painting, *Lu Yu Tasting Tea,* by Zhao Yuan, we see that unlike people in the Tang and Song dynasties who drank tea in studies, courtyards or palaces, people drank tea in mountains or fields, which reflected their broad minds. The anonymous painting *Compatriots with One Mind* in the Yuan Dynasty shows some lovely children drinking tea and baking stuffed buns, and is full of meaning.

In the Ming Dynasty, Zhu Quan, the 17th son of Zhu Yuanzhang, Emperor Taizu, developed Chinese tea art, and became a main representative of naturalistic tea drinkers. Owing to political frustration and complicated conflicts, he became a hermit and devoted himself to founding the naturalistic tea ceremony. Since then, many frustrated scholars have followed him. Among them were poets and painters. For example, the painting *Brewing Tea in Yuchuan* by Ding Yunpeng depicts the scene of tasting tea on a mountain stone beside banana trees under bamboos. Wen Zhengming and Tang Yin (Bohu) of the "four outstanding people in Wuzhong" during the reign of Emperor Jiajing, all painted high-level tea paintings. Wen Zhengming's paintings—*Lu Yu Brewing Tea, Tasting Tea,* and *Tea Gathering in the Huishan*

Mountain—all stress hiding in high mountains and jungles, while Tang Yin's painting *Qin Player* and two paintings entitled *Tasting Tea* are clear, grandiose and varied. All these are rare works in the history of tea paintings.

In the Ming Dynasty, many scholars painted tea paintings, tasted tea in their studies, or drank tea together in bridal chambers. All these reflected certain living conditions and the wide use of tea among common scholars, but, compared with Tang Yin, Wen Zhengming and other master-hands, they are not worth mentioning ideologically or artistically. However, many illustrations in the collected works and novels of the Ming Dynasty, such as the painting of tasting tea in the courtyard, the painting of a lady tasting tea in her boudoir, the painting of tasting tea on a boat in a river with green lotus leaves, reflect the vivid tea culture and the broad social walks of life who engaged in it. The painting *Sweeping Away Snow and Brewing Tea* in the novel *The Plum in the Golden Vase* depicts figures and the scene vividly.

In the Qing Dynasty there were also many tea paintings. Since the ways of making tea were then popular, tea paintings at that time attached importance to teacups and teapots and scenes with a view to reflecting social life rather than the details of brewing tea. In particular, tea paintings at the height of the period, when Kangxi and Qianlong were on the throne, mainly reflected harmony and liveliness. For example, the painting *Spring Market at Peace* by Ding Guanpeng during the reign of Qianlong depicts some even-tempered scholars, who are tasting fragrant tea on nice teasets by pine and plum trees on a broad and beautiful carpet of green grass, and an old man selling tea and fruit passing by with two baskets on his shoulder pole. The painting *Enjoying the Moon* by Leng Mei in the Qing Dynasty shows enjoying the moon and tasting tea in the garden. Tea drinking among common people in the Qing Dynasty was also very popular, a fact reflected in paintings by common people. For example, Yangliuqing woodcuts portray ladies playing cards while tasting tea. Besides this type of work, paintings on appraising tea after Liu Songnian's works and books on the art of tea painting by Mr. Yu Chuan (Lu Tong) were often seen.

In the period of the Republic of China (1912-1949), civic tea culture was practiced on a large scale, and art works on teahouses naturally followed. Tea paintings in books on the art of painting, as well as tea illustrations in novels, were nothing new.

Generally, since the Tang Dynasty, tea was a major subject of painters, who produced many noteworthy works. The special character of tea made it an important way for painters to express their thoughts and feelings. These tea paintings simultaneously inspired tea culture itself, reflecting tea art and tea ceremony in visible forms and deepening people's understanding of its inner secret.

Calligraphy on Tea

The artistic writing of words is called calligraphy. It is not only a technique, but also contains the essence of life, vital energy and spirit. Many calligraphers feel that good calligraphic works are not only a skill gained through long-term cultivation of thought, but also have a lot to do with the state of mind at the time of writing. Tea can keep people sober-minded and make them feel as if they are filling the cosmos. Perhaps just because of this special relationship between tea and calligraphy, many calligraphers like drinking tea. So tea calligraphy which took poems about tea or the word "tea" as its subject became a special preference of painters and calligraphers. Many famous calligraphers had "tea copybooks," or wrote poems on tea in calligraphic form as a way of expressing their art and thoughts.

Tea formed ties with calligraphy very early. Early in the period when Lu Yu created the primary system of Chinese tea culture and compiled *the Book of Tea*, calligraphers took an active part in tea culture activities. Yan Zhenqing, Lu Yu's good friend despite their great difference in age, was well-known as the originator of Yan-style calligraphy. Quite a lot of people knew that Yan was a famous calligrapher, but did not know his official rank or political achievements. After Confucianist Yan Zhenqing made friends with hermit Lu Yu and monk Jiao Ran in Huzhou, they cooperated with each other in many respects, and advocated the combination of tea with calligraphy for the first time. Take the famous Three-Gui Pavilion for example. The pavilion was named for its building on the date, month and year of gui, the last of the ten Heavenly Stems. In Taoism the word "three" implies "bearing everything on earth," while Lu, Jiao and Yan were three persons. According to investigations, Lu Yu designed the pavilion, Jiao Ran wrote a poem for it as a memento, and Yan Zhenqing engraved its history on a stone tablet. These were called three superb works of art. Thus, from the Tang Dynasty, calligraphy on tea officially became an important part of tea culture.

In the Song Dynasty, Emperor Huizong liked tea, poems and calligraphy. He wrote *An Exposition on Tea* and some essays on tea, painted tea paintings, or inscribed poems on tea paintings with the special artistic temperament of a calligrapher. His calligraphy was called thin tendon style. From his painting *Scholars' Gathering,* a superb work of art combining paintings, poems, calligraphy, and tea banquets, we can see his and his ministers' inscribed poems and calligraphy.

In the Ming Dynasty, Tang Yin and Wen Zhengming had a good command of tea art, poems and paintings. Here Zheng Banqiao, one of the "eight strange persons of Yangzhou" in the Qing Dynasty, is noteworthy. He was also called Zheng Xie, and he styled himself Kerou. Born in Xinghua, Jiangsu Province, he was a famous calligrapher, painter and poet, and was, therefore, called a superb person in three aspects. He was especially expert at painting orchids, black bamboo, and strange stones, and his strokes were beautiful and vigorous. His poems strived for realism, freedom and generosity, while his calligraphy blended official script, regular script, cursive script, and grass script. Also, he liked tea. In his poem Prefecture Chief Presenting Tea to Me When I Lived in Yanzhou, he wrote: "The quality tea was given to you by the late ministers Cai Xiang and Ding Wei in Heaven; How should I have thought that you would present it to me?" From this we can see that Zheng Banqiao, as an artist expert at tea, poems and paintings, knew the history of tea very well.

Owing to the special relationship between tea and calligraphy, many great calligraphers wrote special books on calligraphy models of "tea" for appreciation. Some people collected calligraphy models of "tea" to compile a book for comparative study. For example, they put the calligraphy models of "tea," taken from *Xuanmi Tower, Explanation and Study of Principles of Composition of Characters* and works written by such famous calligraphers as Yan Zhenqing, Mi Fu, Xu Wei, Su Guo, Dong Qichang, Zhang Ruitu, Wang Tingjun, Wu Changshuo, Zhao Mengfu, and Zheng Banqiao together in a book on calligraphy models. Although regular script, official script, grass script, seal script, and cursive script were put together on a page, they did not look rigid at all.

Tales About Tea

There were many tales about tea in different parts of China. Some of these tales told of the origin of famous teas with a view to both adding romance to the teas to make them more exalted and publicizing the beauty and prosperity of their hometowns. China was vast in territory and rich in resources, but almost nothing was liked by everyone and eulogized in different tales except tea and liquor. There were tales about grains and plants, such as the tales about the Goddess of Flowers, and the Silkworm Lady Meeting Qiu Hu in the Mulberry Garden. Tea stories, however, were more specific. All famous teas had their own graceful and romantic legends, through which people eulogized famous mountains and rivers, thus making them yearn for and admire famous teas all the more. Tea planters were good at making advertisements for their fine teas through legends. The origin of famous teas accounted for a large proportion of the legends about tea, and every famous tea seemed to have a wonderful history.

Maofeng Tea of Huangshan, Anhui Province, is one famous kind of tea in China, and its Tunxi green tea is praised as "green gold." The first-class Tunxi green tea is also called the treasure of teas, about which there is a beautiful love story. Once there was an orphan named Luo Xiang who lived at the foot of the Huangshan Mountain. The girl, tender as tea and beautiful as flowers, picked delicious tea and sang beautiful songs. High officials, noble lords, scholars, sons of wealthy men, and rich businessmen all proposed marriage to her. Troubled by them, Luo Xiang told her fellow countrymen that she would be engaged through the treasure of teas she had picked. On March 8, at the foot of the Huangshan Mountain, the countrymen, among whom were many rich people and poor people unwilling to be left behind, gathered. Luo Xiang put a table in front of her door, and placed a cup of treasure of teas before each person who proposed marriage to her. She said, "I will choose my husband today, and I hope God will bless me. I have put my vital energy to the tea. The one in whose cup reveals my figure will be my husband." Hearing this, those who proposed marriage to her all watched the tea in the cups before them. But only in the cup set before the woodcutter, Shi Yong, did the fragrant vapors of the tea curl up, in the initial form of a green tea leaf unfolding and later turning into a tea tree. People could see Luo Xiang picking tea under the tree, with the girl inside and outside the cup, as well as the tea in the cup and in the mountain, all becoming an integral whole. As a result, Luo Xiang married the woodcutter. Then the news spread to local authorities. The county magistrate grabbed the treasure of teas from Luo Xiang and presented it to the imperial court. It was fragrant but no soul could be seen in the teacup. So the county magistrate arrested Shi Yong and tortured him to death. However, Luo Xiang saved his life with spring water from the Huangshan Mountain and the treasure of teas, which had a miraculous effect of saving one's life but only with the help of the spring water from the Huangshan Mountain.

Another legend about Maofeng tea of Huangshan is also thought-provoking. During the reign of Tian Qi in the Ming Dynasty there was a learned, refined and incorruptible county magistrate named Xiong Kaiyuan. Once he went to the Yungu Temple in the Huangshan Mountain with his page boy during a spring outing. The elder of the Temple presented him with a kind of fine tea which had sprouts on yellow leaves which looked like white hair. He made tea with the boiling water from a Huangshan Mountain spring, and found that not only did the tea have unparalleled color, fragrance and taste, but when it changed and rose, the wonder of a white lotus appeared in the air. According to the elder, when the Holy Farmer got poisoned after tasting herbs, the Tea Fairy and the Huangshan Mountain God saved his life with the tea. Out of gratitude, the Holy Farmer left them a holy seat of lotus; so drinking this kind of tea naturally promised good health and longevity. Later, a county magistrate who madly desired an official position secretly presented the tea to the emperor so his meritorious deeds could be recorded. But since he did not know that the white lotus would not appear without the spring water from the Huangshan Mountain, he harmed himself in his greed for recognition. Seeing through the corruption of officials, Xiong Kaiyuan resigned and became a monk at the Yungu Temple, accompanied all day by Maofeng tea, spring water and his roommates. Superficially, there seems to be no difference between this story and ordinary folktales, but a careful study proves that it is not the case. First, included in it is the story of the Holy Farmer's tasting herbs, which repeats the lore that tea was used early in the Holy Farmer's time. Second, the legend that the white lotus would appear if tea was made with the spring water reflects the relationship between Buddhism, which revered the lotus, and tea. Elder Huineng and Xiong Kaiyuan, an elegant Confucianist, practiced tea ceremony together at the Yungu Temple, which demonstrates that a real tea connoisseur must be a detached and virtuous man. As for the county magistrate who was always flattering the emperor, he had nothing to do with the graceful moral character of Maofeng tea of Huangshan. This ordinary folktale reflects many problems and shows the implications and depth of folk art.

However, in the legends about tea there is more a flavor of fairies than of Buddhism. Fairies impress the Chinese people more than Buddhism does, for fairies, who are alive, stand for beauty and wisdom, qualities which are pursued by the Chinese people, especially laborers. Taiping Houkui tea in Anhui Province was, according to a folktale, given by two old monkeys which had attained the Way. But some people say that it was cultivated by a beautiful girl named Hou Kui with all her energy. Making tea with the Hou Kui tea leaves, one can see smoke curling up out of the teapot, and the figures of his family members in the smoke. There are also many legends about the Red Robe tea of the Wuyi

Mountain. According to some, in a year with poor harvest in the Wuyi Mountain, an old and kind-hearted Lady Qin saved an old immortal man, who later inserted a stick into the earth and the stick became a tea tree. Afterwards, the emperor dug up the tea tree and planted it in his palace. But the fairylike tea tree rose sharply from the ground and flew to the Wuyi Mountain. Its red leaves were the flowing colored clouds, as well as the robe of the tea fairy. Some people, however, say that the emperor bestowed red robes on three tea trees, for the tea cured the queen of a disease. It should be noted here that many legends about famous tea include moving love stories about the treatment of disease. This theme stressed the medical value of tea and its pure moral character. An interesting legend about Junshan tea of the Dongting Lake tells of an old Taoist priest who gave advice to the queen mother of the State of Chu. The old queen mother was always falling ill, and the filial devotion of her son, king of the State, moved Heaven. An old Taoist priest with a white beard came to treat her. But he said that nothing was wrong with her except that she ate so many delicacies from land and sea that she was suffering from stomach trouble. Before taking his leave, he left a gourd of divine water, along with the following true sentences:

Two decoctions a day, and more vegetables each meal;
If you want a long life, walk a hundred paces after supper.

The queen mother recovered; but a high official of the state wanted to remove the divine water of Junshan Mountain to the royal palace. Angered at this, the old Taoist priest sprayed the Junshan Mountain with a pond of divine water, which turned into thousands of tea trees as effectual as the divine water. The king of the State of Chu blamed the old Taoist priest for the crime of "deception on the King," but the priest said that if the King had cleaned out the divine water, he had committed the crime of "deception on the people," for each place had its own way of supporting its own inhabitants. The king had to give in. From then on, he sent a hundred girls in red to pick tea in the Junshan Mountain every year. The girls, twenty in each group, were like flowers dotted on the rippling green mountain. Seeing the beautiful scenery, the king was in an exalted, poetic mood. "In the vast expanse of green bushes, the girls in red are picking tea leaves...." Chanting at this, he suddenly realized that in the Chinese character "tea," the symbol for "person" is between those for "grass" and "wood," and the original complex form of the stroke "grass" could also be written as a simplified form of the word "twenty," which was the way that the girls were organized into teams. Why did the King insist on removing the divine spring of the Junshan Mountain, since everything has its own natural reason? Cleverly contrived, the story satirized and gave advice to the rulers, and brought out the theme in the end with a maxim: After drinking a cup of tea, the King should be sober-minded, not taking too much or troubling the people too much.

That good tea is made with good water is the basic requirement of tea art. On this point the common people are the most qualified to speak, for they often live beside famous waters rather than assiduously seeking after them. Many stories exist about the discovery and protection of famous springs and waters. For example, the Hupao Spring in Hangzhou is said to have been dug out with superhuman strength by two brothers called Dahu and Erhu, who became tigers in order to save the local people.

In Guilin, Guangxi Zhuang Autonomous Region, there is a tale about the White Dragon Spring and Liu Xianyan tea. It is said that the tea made with the water from the White Dragon Spring was fragrant, and out of the vapor flew a white dragon. So the water was treated as a tribute specially paid to the Emperor. The Liu Xianyan tea is said to have been planted by an immortal called Liu

Jing in the Song Dynasty. In fact, the so-called immortal was simply a living human being who had attained the Way. We can see from these examples that legends about tea and springs are simply twists on real life.

Some stories reproduce historical facts in a way people love to hear and talk about. Here is the story about an exchange of a horse for *The Book of Tea*. In the last years of the Tang Dynasty, monarchs set up separate regimes by force of arms and rebelled against the imperial court. The Emperor was badly in need of horses to put down these rebellions, so the imperial court exchanged tea for horses with the State of Huihe. In the autumn of that year, messengers from both the Tang Dynasty and the State of Huihe met again at the border. This time the messenger from the State of Huihe wanted to exchange a thousand strong horses for *The Book of Tea*. The author of the book, Lu Yu, however, had died, and the book was not yet universally known. So the Emperor ordered his messengers to use all possible means to search for the book in Tiaoxi, Huzhou, where the author wrote the book, and his home county Jingling (today's Tianmen County, Hubei Province). At last the great poet Pi Rixiu took out a manuscript, which was later exchanged for the horses. From then on *The Book of Tea* was spread abroad. Irrespective of whether the story derived from the common people or from scholars, it was cleverly invented, for it linked the exchange of tea for horses with the spread of *The Book of Tea*. In fact, the Tang Government kept in frequent contact with the State of Huihe, for it was in the Tang Dynasty that *The Book of Tea* was spread to the northwest part of our country. This story gives us an important clue for the study of the history of tea culture in the northwest.

According to one legend, there is a big camellia in the Luliang County, Yunnan Province. It was more than two *zhang* (6.6 meters) tall and one arm span around, and each of its flowers had nine stamens and eighteen petals. People called it the King of Camellias. The legend about the tree, however, is linked with the history of Wu Sangui's governing of Yunnan. It is said that because Wu Sangui plotted to be Emperor after having dominated Yunnan, he built a palace in the Wuhua Mountain and the Axiang Garden by the Lotus Pool, and searched everywhere for exotic flowers and rare herbs. Then he forced the transplantation of King of Camellias in Luliang County to his palace. It turned out that the tree had an iron will, growing leaves but not coming into flower, in spite of scars of the wounds inflicted on it by Wu Sangui's whip. Three years later, Wu Sangui wanted to kill the gardener in a fury. Then the tea fairy came into his dream, singing:

> *"Don't be drunk, Sangui.*
> *The gardener is innocent,*
> *but you are mistaken.*
> *As a girl from a peasant family,*
> *I don't seek wealth and rank.*
> *I only wish to go home*
> *And spend the rest of my life."*

Hearing this, Wu Sangui wielded his sword, but instead of killing the tea fairy, he cut off the dragon's head of a dragon chair. Then he heard the tea fairy singing:

> *"Mean, low and notorious,*
> *You have betrayed your master for glory.*
> *You disreputable gang is completely absorbed in*
> *Building your palace,*
> *With your throne stained with blood.*
> *Since what you did has caused*
> *Widespread indignation and discontent,*
> *Ghosts will haunt you and punish you."*

Hearing this, Wu Sangui was dizzy, and broke out in a cold sweat all over from fear. Suddenly he woke up and found that he was having a dream in Nanke. Fearing of the haunting of ghosts, his adviser suggested that he "relegate" the King of Camellias to Luliang County. This story mainly illustrates the inflexible character of tea by cleverly quoting the historical fact that Wu Sangui rose in rebellion and declared himself Emperor. Actually, there are many such historical stories in Yunnan. For example, many stories tell of Zhuge Liang, who taught people how to plant and use tea, directly stressing the blending of foreign culture with Chinese culture. Zhuge Liang was also known as Kong Ming, so in many places in Yunnan Province, people call some big tea trees "Kong Ming Trees." We do not know whether people in Yunnan learned to plant and use tea only after Kong Ming reached Yunnan. But spiritually, people of different nationalities value historical figures for different reasons.

Some stories, whether made up by scholars or by common people, sound interesting. For example, the story about "serving tea according to loneliness and nobleness" is of great interest. Zheng Banqiao, a great painter and calligrapher, as well as one of the "Eight Strange Persons" in the Qing Dynasty, always pursued his studies in Zhenjiang. One day he went to the abbot's room in the Jinshan Temple to enjoy calligraphy. At first, the snobbish abbot did not even glance at Zheng Banqiao, who was in plain clothes. He reluctantly told Zheng to sit down. Then he said to the little monk attending, "Tea!" During their talk, the abbot learned that Zheng and he were from the same town, so he said, "Please sit down!" Then he cried to the little monk, "Serve tea!" But when he learned that the visitor was the well- known Zheng Banqiao, he was so delighted that he said quickly, "Please take the seat of honor!" And he hurriedly ordered the little monk, "Serve fragrant tea!" Having drunk tea, Zheng stood up and was about to take his leave.

Then the old monk asked Zheng to bestow on him some couplets or treasured scrolls of calligraphy or paintings. Zheng waved his hand and wrote the first line, "Sit down, please sit down, please take the seat of honor!" And the second line was, "Tea, serve tea, serve fragrant tea!" This pair of couplets fitted wonderfully, the words matching well, and had a strong ironical flavor. Another story tells of Zhu Yuanzhang, who bestowed a cap and belt on a waiter in a teahouse. Once, the founder of the Ming Dynasty, Zhu Yuanzhang, was inspecting the state institution of higher learning after an evening banquet. A cook presented him with a cup of scented tea. It happened that Zhu was thirsty at the time. The more he drank the tea, the more fragrant he felt the tea was. So he granted the cook a cap and belt on a sudden impulse. Unimpressed by this, a tribute student in the yard sang loudly, "Ten years of studies in spite of hardships is no match for a small cup of tea." All were surprised at the tribute student's offending the Emperor. But Zhu said the second line with a smile, "He has less knowledge than you, but you have a worse fate than he." The story showed Zhu's liking for tea. Also, it is consistent with history. Being of low origin, Zhu was considerate of laborers. And since he almost had no schooling, he laid stress only on practice to the neglect of knowledge.

Chapter 7
Tea and Social Rites

Folk customs, an important component part of national culture, showed the psychological characteristics of a nation. In the past, they had distinctive local features. It is truly said that "Ten *li* apart, but the customs are quite different." Customs were colorful and varied in attitude, which is often ignored. However, they reflected profound cultural psychologies. The same is true of tea-drinking. Although popular drinking methods were not as standardized as the Confucian, Taoist and Buddhist tea culture systems, most of the common people carried out the spirit of tea culture in their work, clothing, food, shelter and transportation, various social rites such as weddings and funerals, and social intercourse, showing that the spirit of Chinese tea culture was integrated with the thoughts of the common people.

Tea Rites in Daily Life

It was a popular Chinese custom to entertain one's guest with tea to show great respect to him. People in different areas had various ways of serving tea.

Wealthy and influential families in North China (the Huanghe River Valley and the region north of it) served their guests with three courses of tea. The host first led the guest to the central room.

After greeting each other, the host would ask their servants or children to serve tea. The first course of tea, which was presented when the guest had just arrived, served only as a formality. The guest either left it untouched or took a sip. The second course was served as host and guest talked animatedly with each other. The guest tasted the wonderful tea carefully. They talked while drinking, exchanging their feelings. The third course was served after they had finished talking, and the tea had become weak. The guest then took his leave, and the host saw him off. However, close friends did not adhere to these formalities when they wanted to talk to their hearts' content.

People in regions south of the Yangtze River have entertained guests with the best tea and food to give blessing and show respect to them since the Song and Yuan dynasties. Hunan people entertained guests with tea containing fried soya beans, sesame and ginger slices. Besides drinking the tea, the guests chewed beans, sesame and tea leaves. Instead of using chopsticks, they patted the rims of teacups to suck the tasty morsels out. Villagers in Hubei Province drank plain water at ordinary times, and entertained guests with tea made of popcorn. Sometimes they added malt and tinosporaes to show special respect to their guests. In regions south of the Yangtze River, people offered their guests *yuanbao* tea during the Spring Festival to wish them luck and bring wealth and treasures in the coming year. It was made of Chinese olives or kumquats which had been cut open, and looked like *yuanbao* (a shoe-shaped gold ingot).

People entertained guests with tea, or presented it as a gift to their relatives or friends. During the Song Dynasty, people in Kaifeng were very righteous and warm-hearted. They often helped the bullied non-natives. When a resident moved into a new house, the neighbors offered him tea, or invited him to go to their homes to drink tea to show their friendliness and care. The tea was called *zhicha*. The Southern Song Dynasty later moved the capital to Hangzhou, and this good tradition was caried there. The custom of showing one's friendliness and respect to a guest by offering tea has been preserved up to the present. Every family in Hangzhou City, Zhejiang Province, presented newly-made tea and excellent fruits as gifts to their relatives and friends at the Beginning of Summer (7th solar term). The custom, called *qijiacha*, was handed down from the Song Dynasty, and recorded in a book written during the Ming Dynasty. According to the *Records of Chinese Customs*, people of the State of *Wu* sought tea from their neighbors, and brewed it with the previous year's charcoal at the Beginning of Summer. This, too, was called *qijiacha*.

Tea was used not only to serve guests, but also to show mutual respect and love among family members, and the feudal order of importance or seniority in human relationships. As far back as the Song and Yuan dynasties, it was an important component of family rites to serve tea to the family elder. The Chinese stressed genetic connection, family relationship, and advocated respect for aged people and protection of the young. In the old China, children of a wealthy and influential family gave morning greetings to their parents, and the oldest son or daughter served them a cup of newly brewed scented tea on behalf of the other children. The custom was more popular in South China. A bride had to get up early and serve newly brewed scented tea to her parents-in-law when she greeted them on the second wedding morning. The rite was designed to show three things: the bride's filial respect for her parents-in-law; keeping early hours and being industrious and thrifty in running her home; and being clever and deft. In the land of tea, a young married woman who could not brew and serve tea was regarded as clumsy and unreasonable.

Well-off families in Jiangxi Province followed a fixed rule when drinking tea. Servants, long-term hired hands and sedan-chair bearers drank tea from *baohu*, a huge tin teapot covered with cotton and put in a large vat. They tipped it to pour out the tea through a little hole in the vat. Ordinary family members and guests drank tea from *tenghu*, a smaller china pot in a cane container. The master of the house or distinguished guests coming on festival days were served newly brewed tea in teacups with covers. It reflected obsession of hierarchy, and respect for seniority.

The Han tea rite was spread to ethnic minorities. In the Dali Area where the Bai ethnic group lived, each family drank tea while admiring the beauty of flowers at every festival and at New Year. They built small gardens, or grew trees and flowers or potted plants in the courtyards or on the steps. They sometimes invited their friends to brew tea while admiring the beauty of flowers. A child had to learn to serve tea to its parents or guests. The first test for a bride was to see whether she could rise early, and serve tea to her parents-in-law before they got up to show her filial respect for them. If she could, she would be regarded as industrious and deft; otherwise, she would be regarded as lazy, clumsy and ill-bred. It was the main spirit of the Chinese family tea rite to show respect for one's elders by serving them tea. Although the family tea rite in feudal societies contained some negative factors such as the view that men were superior to women, it advocated that people should respect the old and cherish the young, live with each other in harmony, and be industrious and thrifty in running their homes.

Wedding Customs and Tea Rite

The tea rite was most widely reflected in wedding customs. Compared with Westerners, the Chinese attached greater importance to genetic connections, and regarded marriage as the most important event of their lives. The tea rite was reflected in wedding customs, for tea represented purity, firmness, and the view that the more children one had, the happier one would be. The Chinese regarded tea as the purest thing, symbolizing pure and noble love between men and women. The ancients believed that transplanted tea could not survive (people have now mastered the skill), so tea was sometimes called *buqian* (unmovable) to express unswerving love. As tea had many seeds, it symbolized the Chinese view that the more children and grandchildren one had, the happier one would be. So, when combined with marriage systems, the tea rite became one of the most important rites of one's life.

In South China among Han people, on an engagement, the bridegroom-to-be offered betrothal gifts to the bride's family, an action which was called *xiachali* (offering tea). The wedding custom called *sanchali* (three tea rites) in regions south of the Yangtze River can be explained in two ways: It may refer to three courtesies on the engagement and wedding ceremony of a new couple: that is, *xiachali* on the engagement, *dingchali* on the wedding ceremony, and "*hechali*" on the first wedding night. It may, however, refer to the three tea courses of the wedding ceremony: the first course, ginkgos; the second, lotus seeds and dates; and the third, tea. In both explanations, tea symbolized pure and unswerving love.

Tea was first used in weddings as far back as the Song Dynasty. The bridegroom presented tea as a betrothal gift to the bride's family when he made an offer of marriage, which was called "knocking at the door." The matchmaker was also called "the person carrying tea caddies." On the day before the marriage, the bride's family went to the bridegroom's house to decorate the bridal curtain and chamber, and offer them tea and wine. In *The Peony Pavilion* written by Tang Xianzu, the father said, "My daughter died three years ago. No man had ever presented tea as a gift and made an offer of marriage, and she had never been engaged to anyone before she was born." As described in *The Peach Blossom Fan* written by Kong Shangren, "The bridal sedan chair was ready to carry the bride to the bridegroom's house, and the bridegroom's family has offered adequate tea as a betrothal gift." In *A Dream of Red Mansions*, Wang Xifeng said to Lin Daiyu, "Since you have drunk our family's tea, you should marry into our family." These quotations show that tea was a time-honored symbol of marriage. Tea was essential in the old wedding custom in Jiangsu Province. The matchmaker   passed the card containing the hour, date, month and year of the bride's birth written in red golden paint, and the bridegroom's side offered tea, fruits, gold and silver as betrothal gifts. On the wedding day, the bridegroom went horse-riding to the bride's home with a sedan chair and waited at the gate. He had to make a bow with his hands folded in front of him whenever he entered a door until he reached the central room, and greeted his father-in-law and the honored guests. After he was served three courses of tea, he went to his mother-in-law's room to wait for the bride to enter the sedan chair. It was called "tea served when opening the door."

Tea occupied an important place in wedding ceremonies in Hunan and Jiangxi provinces, known as famous tea production areas. As the saying goes in Liuyang City and other places, "young men and women would pledge to marry by drinking tea together." If the young man and woman agreed to meet each other, the matchmaker would lead the young man to the girl's home on a fixed day. If the girl agreed to associate with him, she would serve him a cup of tea. If the man was satisfied, he would leave payment for tea in the cup; otherwise he would also drink tea to show his respect to the young woman, then place the cup on the table upside down. The payment for tea should be even in number, ranging from two to 100 yuan. If the man drank the tea, the marriage would have hope of success. Young men and women in Hunan Province showed their reactions to each other by drinking tea and eating eggs. If the girl went to the man's home, and the man was satisfied with her, he would offer her three or more eggs; if he was not, he offered only two eggs. The girl would show her good faith by eating the three or more eggs happily. If the man went to the girl's home, and the girl was satisfied with him, she would offer him tea and eggs; if not, only tea.

The tea rite on the engagement in Hunan Province was unique in style. The bridegroom's side went to the bride's home to offer betrothal gifts including *yanchapan*—a plate on which displayed patterns such as "the luan (a mythical bird likes a phoenix) and the phoenix," and "the magpie carrying a plum branch in its bill." The patterns were made of dyed lampwicks, and the space between filled with tea and salt. The custom was called *zhengcha*. (formal tea). If the bride's family accepted it, the marriage would be settled, and both of them could never go back on their word.

In Hunan Province, the bridegroom and bride would meet their seniors and offer them scented tea when guests took their seats after the wedding ceremony. Each senior would put a red paper containing money on the tea tray after he or she drank tea. In some areas, the bridegroom and bride drank tea together on the wedding night, just as newly married couples in North China drank "cross-cupped wine" from one another's glasses. When the bride entered the bridal chamber, the bridegroom offered the bride a cup of tea with both hands. The bride took a sip, then the bridegroom followed. Thus they completed the most solemn ceremony in their lives.

It was a popular Chinese custom to celebrate weddings in the bridal chamber. People in Hunan Province held merriments centered around tea, such as *hehecha* and *chitaicha*. *Hehecha* was recorded in the *Records of Chinese Customs*, and it is still popular in many places. The bridegroom and bride sat on the same bench,

113

facing each other, and putting their left legs on the other's right legs. The bridegroom put his left hand on the bride's shoulder, and the bride put her right hand on the bridegroom's shoulder. Then they closed their thumbs and index fingers of their free hands to form a square. They held a cup filled with tea in the "square," then people drank tea from it in turn. *Taicha* was another custom. The newly married couple carried a tea tray on which were placed cups filled with tea, and asked guests to drink tea in turn. Every guest should speak words of praise before they drank tea; if he could not think of praise, he had to give up his turn to the next guest. In some areas, the newly married couples offered both tea and eggs to their seniors. The seniors then gave them red paper containing money as a gift.

The tea rite of weddings in Huzhou Area, Zhejiang Province, was similar to that of Hunan and Jiangxi provinces. The acceptance of the betrothal presents offered by the bridegroom's side was called *chicha* (drinking tea) or *shoucha* (accepting tea); the newly married couple offered tea to show respect to their seniors. The gifts given by the seniors were called *chabao*. In North China, the bride returned to her mother's home on the third day of the wedding, which was called *huimen*, while in some areas of Zhejiang Province, the bride's parents went to see their daughter on the third day, which was called *wangzhao*. The parents would bring 0.5 *jin* of dry beans, flavedo, sesame and tea gathered before Grain Rain (the 6th solar term) to the bridegroom's home to make tea. The two families talked while drinking, which was called *qingjiapocha*. (tea offered by the bride's mother)

Once the couple had borne sons and daughters tea played a different role. In Huzhou Area, Zhejiang Province, a baby had its head shaved on the completion of its first month of life, and its head was washed with tea to wish it intellgence, and to bring it a long life of abundance and respectability. The custom was called *chayu kaishi*.

The Bai ethnic group in Dali County, Yunnan Province, lived at the foot of Mount Cangshan by Erhai Lake, tea's birthplace. Tea's spirit was reflected in the area's wedding custom. Young girls were skillful in baking tea. They stewed water on an iron tripod mounted in the central room, and baked tea in a small sand jar by its side. Then they poured boiling water on the baked tea when it sent out an enchanting fragrance. Foams rose from the mouth of the jar like rounded pincushions. One of the standards by which the bride was appraised was whether she could offer such wonderful baked tea to her parents-in-law. The bridegroom's fellows and juniors celebrated the wedding in the bridal chamber, and the newly married couple offered them three courses of tea, which was different from that served at ordinary times. The first course was bitter tea instead of sugar tea; the second, sweet tea with brown sugar and nuts; and the third, milk tea made with cheese and brown sugar. "The first course was bitter; the second, sweet; and the third would lead a person to endless aftertastes." There was much philosophy of life in the custom.

The king of tea in Menghai County, Yunnan Province, was well known both at home and abroad. It was a local custom that the bride climbed the tree to gather tea. The local people believed that the higher she climbed, and the more tea she gathered, the luckier the couple would be. The bridegroom might feel embarrassed to tell a stranger the reason for the custom, but if questioned closely over and over again, he would finally tell: "We gathered tea from the king of tea so that it would bless us to have a lasting affection towards each other, exuberant vitality, and many children just as itself does." If a guest happened to visit them, the newly married couple would knead and bake the tea, and offer him fragrant tea to show their respect.

The Lahu ethnic group living by the Lancangjiang River enjoyed freedom of marriage. Young couples had some experience before they got married, such as exploration, singing in antiphonal style, scrambling for turbans, secret meetings and stabilizing the passions. When a couple were attracted to each other, they would pledge to marry, and finally tell their parents. The bridegroom's side asked a matchmaker to go to the bride's home to make an offer of marriage. The matchmaker presented a pair of candles, cigarettes, tea and other things as betrothal gifts on behalf of the bridegroom, among which tea was an essential item. The Lahu people believed that if the bridegroom did not offer tea, the marriage would not count. After the formal wedding ceremony, the bridge and bridegroom carried water and offered it to their parents and the matchmaker. Such a marriage would be regarded as a happy marriage.

Tea had an important place in the wedding ceremony of the Maonan ethnic group in the northwest of Guangxi Zhuang Autonomous Region. On the wedding day, after the man sent by the bridegroom's side had lunch at the bride's home, the bride's family started to "fold the quilt." The bride's mother filled a large copper pen with red eggs, polished glutinous rice, icker, tangerines, melon seeds, copper cash, and tea—an essential item. The bride's sister(s)-in-law and aunt(s) folded the quilt into a square, and placed it on a yoke called *gang*, with a copper pen on one end, and a tin teapot on the other, and draped with many cloth shoes made by the bride. The practice of "transforming marriage" was popular in the Maonan ethnic group. When an elder brother died, the younger one would marry his wife, or vice versa. The ceremony was called "transforming tea."

In the Achang ethnic group, the matchmaker went to the bride's home to offer two bags of tea, tobacco and sugar. On the third day of the wedding, when the bride's family went to the bridegroom's home to send her dowry and "large lunch-box," the bridegroom's family proposed a toast, "Please ride the large white horse;" and another toast on departure, "Please ride the large red horse to return home!"

The wedding custom of the Qiang ethnic group in the Aba area of Sichuan Province was very interesting. As a special local product, tea was an essential wedding gift. On the wedding day, three gun salute was fired whenever the contingents of people who go to the bride's home to escort her to the wedding passed a village. Villagers went out to see the fun. The relatives of the bridegroom and the bride entertained the contingents with tea and food made of corn, highland barley, wheat and soya beans. They moved on after drinking and eating. In this way, they showed their blessings and friendship. Finally, the bride reached the bridegroom's home.

Besides showing faithfulness and respect, ethnic groups in the northwest of China showed their wealth through the tea rite at weddings. Tea was essential in their daily life, but was hard to come by. In the Sala ethnic group in Qinghai, the bridegroom's side asked the matchmaker to go to the bride's home on an auspicious day to offer a pair of earrings and a package of *fucha* tea as "engagement tea"; the custom was called *xiding*. In the Bonan ethnic group in Gansu Province, the bridegroom's father or uncle, and the matchmaker went to the bride's home to offer a pair of earrings, two packages of *fucha* tea and some clothes. The Yugu ethnic group valued tea highly. Before liberation, a lump of *fucha* tea had to be exchanged for two sheep. The bridegroom had to offer a horse, an ox, more than ten sheep, 20 pieces of cloth, and two lumps of *fucha* tea to the bride's family. Match-making was called *shuocha* in the Hui ethnic group. Parents of both sides took a look at their prospective daughter- or son-in-law on such a meeting. If the bridegroom's parents took a fancy to the bride, the matchmaker would go to her home to bring back words and offer *fucha* tea. If the bride's side agreed, they would accept the tea. Thus they were engaged to each other. The rite was called *dingcha* (betrothal tea) or *xicha* (wedding tea). The bride's family divided the tea into small pieces, and gave it to their relatives, friends and neighbors as presents.

Tea also had an important place in Tibetan wedding customs. Tibetans enjoyed freedom in love. Young men and women measured their future husband or wife by his or her appearance and moral standings instead of family financial situation and betrothal gifts. They sang songs when they pledged to marry, using tea as a metaphor for love:

Could we eat *zanba* in our bags together?

Could we brew tea in our pots together?

Could we exchange our golden bracelets and silver rings?

Could we exchange our long and short belts?

From this pledge, we can see that Tibetans regarded tea as important as golden bracelets and silver belts. Buttered tea was also essential for a wedding.

The Man ethnic group developed from the Nüzhen ethnic group in Heilongjiang Province. Tea was used in their wedding ceremonies as far back as the Jin Dynasty. At that time, they still preserved the remnants of a matriarchal system, and a man's proposal was called *xiachali* (offering tea). On the wedding day, the bride's family sat on a *kang* (a raised heated platform used for sleeping) to receive the kowtows of the bridegroom's family. Then they drank tea and ate candied fruits together. In the Qing Dynasty, the Man ethnic group continued this old custom. They also called an engagement *xiachali*, although it was a simplified form of the earlier custom.

Tea was widely used in weddings of many Chinese ethnic groups. It had an important place in wedding customs in the Central Plains and border areas, southwest, northwest and northeast China. It showed that people everywhere believed that tea was the symbol of firmness, purity, love and luck.

Funeral and Sacrificial Customs and Tea Rites

Tea has been used in funerals and sacrificial rites for a long time. According to a story in *The Book of Tea* quoted from *Strange Tales*—(a collection of strange tales from the pre-Qin period written by Liu Jingshu in the State of Song (420-479) during the Southern Dynasties (420-589)—Chen Wu's widow lived with two sons when she was still young. The family loved sampling tea, and often offered tea as a sacrificial offering to a ghost, for there was an old tomb near their house. The sons wanted to open the tomb, and Chen Wu's widow tried hard to persuade them to give up the idea. At night, she dreamt that the ghost came to thank her: "I have lived here for more than 300 years. Your two sons wanted to destroy the tomb. Fortunately, you protected me, and often offered me excellent tea. I will pay you a debt of gratitude!" They found 100,000 cash the next day. It might be the earliest record of using tea as a sacrificial offering.

Archaeological discoveries have proved the custom of using tea as a funerary object. For example, a box of tea was found in the famous Tombs of the Han Dynasty at Mawangdui in Changsha City, Hunan Province. The murals in the Tombs of the Liao Dynasty (907-1125) in Xuanhua City, Hebei Province, vividly depict the scene of making and drinking tea. The Chinese regarded death as the end of their lives, and wished to continue their lives after they died. They believed that they could be reborn after death, although they contradicted themselves by also imagining life in the underworld. Therefore, tea became a funerary object so that people could continue drinking in the after-life.

However, there were many far-fetched superstitious stories about popular funeral customs. It was widely believed in China that ghosts in the nether world would compel a person who had just died drink a magic potion to make him forget all the past on earth,

119

or lead him into a maze so that the ghosts could humiliate and enslave him. The Chinese believed that one should be reasonable and sober, and it was unwise to drink the magic potion. Tea could help people keep a clear head. So tea became an important component part of funeral customs in many tea producing areas. According to the *Records of Chinese Customs*, people in Zhejiang Province and some other areas believed that "besides a silver ingot, the family of the deceased should put a *ling* made of mannan leaves in his mouth, and a pack of tea in his hand so that he could not be filled with the magic potion. They would mutter Buddhist scriptures when they laid the coffin: 'He was holding mannan leaves, and could eat juicy pink *ling* when he felt thirsty.'" This custom was also popular in Anhui Province. It was not only applied to the dead, but also to the living. Necromancy was popular in Jiangsu Province. When a child was ill, a man held his clothes on a balance, and another man carried a lantern. They echoed each other's utterances, and sprinkled rice and tea while walking so that ghosts could not entice the child's lost soul. The ceremony was called "calling home the lost soul."

Tea was rare in North China, so it was not often used in funerals. However, it was widely used in sacrificial rites to ghosts, spirits or ancestors. It is interesting to note that the Chinese believed that everything had a spirit so there were mountain gods, water gods, town gods, local gods of the land, tree gods, grain gods, flower gods and insect goddesses. The door god and kitchen god were regarded as the most important gods of a family. The door god, transformed from a hero in history, blessed and protected peaceful family life. It is said that a sacrificial rite to the kitchen god was held throughout China on the 23rd of the twelfth month of the lunar year in commemoration of the date when he went up to the sky. The Chinese were disrespectful to gods sometimes. For example, people made fun of the kitchen god. On the 23rd of the twelfth month of the lunar year, each family tried to bribe him with *zaotang*, which was called *tanggua* (candied melons) in North China, so that he would not inform secretly on them in heaven. In the Liaoyang area of northeast China, every family made a pony with gaoliang (Chinese songhum) shafts so that the kitchen god could ride it to go up to the sky. At night, they offered a cup of tea and a cup of hay. Some people held that the tea was given to the pony, while others insisted that it was prepared for the kitchen god. It was difficult to be the kitchen god, for he had to "give compliments to people when he was in heaven, and when on earth, bless and protect them to live peacefully."

Although these customs were fatuous and superstitious, they also contained Chinese philosophies of life. The Chinese advocated that people should look squarely at life when they were alive, instead of leading a befuddled life as if drunk or in a dream; when they died, they should strive to control their own lives instead of being ordered about by ghosts and gods at will. People used tea in funerals and sacrificial rites because tea could help them keep a clear head.

Chapter 8
Folk Tea Art

Ancient Customs of Huzhou

Huzhou Prefecture, Zhejiang Province, China, is an old tea growing area, where the Saint of Tea Lu Yu wrote *The Book of Tea*. In the ranges of green mountains with their clear streams, lakes and rivers, the rich soil here is suitable for growing tea trees. More important, many different forms of ancient tea art, which can be called typical tea ceremonies among the common people, have been preserved intact.

Nowadays, the Huzhou people are particular about the procedures of making tea, which mainly include welcoming the guests, setting teasets on the table, boiling water, pouring boiling water into the teapot, stirring the tea in teacups, serving tea, tasting tea, seeing the guests off, and several other procedures. Before guests come, the hostess gets everything ready, such as fine tea, condiments, fruit, clean teasets, clear water and bamboo sticks. When the guests enter the door, the hostess lets them sit in the seat of honor. The hostess hangs up a special pot for boiling water, which can be treated as the variant of Lu Yu's "tea boiler," and uses thin bamboo splints as firewood. When the water boils, the hostess takes out small bags of tender tea leaves, and pours them into the bowl pinch by pinch. Then she grasps a handful of dry, pickled and cooked green soybeans, grips other condiments on the table with chopsticks, and then puts them into the bowl. At this time she pours the boiling water in the pot into the bowl, filling 70 percent of it, and stirs with chopsticks. Drinking tea in this way is a custom handed down from the Tang Dynasty. In later periods, to keep the fragrance of tea, scholars and the upper class no longer drank tea like this, but the common people carried on as before.

At the moment when the flavors of tea and condiments are mingled in the water, a fragrant smell strikes the nose. It is the best time to drink. So, the hostess holds the cups of tea before the guests respectfully and skillfully, saying, "Please drink tea." Then she takes out nuts and melon seeds, and puts them on the center of the table. After that, the hostess and the guests drink and eat as they talk. The tea made with dried green soybeans is salty. Generally speaking, the tea, condiments and green soybeans are eaten together after the boiling water has been added to the tea three times. Then the hostess makes new tea again.

This kind of tea art is just like a beautiful poem, making you feel the freshness of the tea and the friendship between the hostess and the guests during the course of boiling, serving and drinking tea. In Huzhou Prefecture, no respect for guests can be shown without serving tea like this.

The tea tasting party of Huzhou Prefecture further shows the connotations of this tea ceremony. Here married women, old or young, have a special get-together each year to taste tea. Perhaps this is an old custom handed down from the tea parties of Lu Yu and Jiao Ran.

Taking a panoramic view of the tea ceremony of Huzhou Prefecture, we can see that there are many similarities between the tea ceremony of Huzhou Prefecture and that of ancient China: 1. The tea art has certain rules, the first of all the rules is to create the atmosphere of drinking tea through graceful manipulation.

2. The ancient custom of adding condiments to tea is preserved.

3. Unlike the way of drinking tea in north China, in which tea is poured into cups from a big teapot, tea is made in teacups on the spot.

4. After the boiling water is poured to the tea, the tea must be stirred vigorously. This is similar to the common tea ceremonies of the Yuan and Ming dynasties.

5. The tea ceremony emphasizes more respect for guests rather than the quenching of thirst.

6. The ancient tea party is preserved, with the tea party of Huzhou being a typical tea ceremony of the common people.

7. Unlike ancient hermits, Taoist priests or Buddhist monks, the Chinese love life, like social intercourse and enjoy sharing joys, which is fully expressed by the tea ceremony.

The Kong Fu Tea of Chaozhou and Shantou

There are different opinions about the name of kong fu tea. Some people think that it is called thus because it takes a lot of time to process the tea leaves; some think that it derives its name because it takes a long time to taste mouthful by mouthful this strong and bitter tea contained in tiny teacups; and some think that it is so called because it stresses the method of tasting and needs special operating skills. All these opinions seem reasonable, but the third one is the most rational.

Kong fu tea is popular in Fujian and Guangdong provinces and other places southeast of China. Now let's take the Chaozhou and Shantou kong fu tea as an example.

The Chaozhou and Shantou kong fu tea has an integrated ceremony encompassing the reflected spirit, the etiquette, the skills of both making tea and pouring tea for guests, and the appraisal of the quality of the tea.

Generally speaking, there are altogether four people, including the host or hostess, in a Chaozhou and Shantou kong fu tea ceremony. This limitation of the number of the people is similar to the ideas of the tea drinkers of the Ming and Qing dynasties, who thought that tea drinkers should keep quiet, have few desires and share the same views. Starting from the right side of the host or hostess, the guests sit on both sides of the table according to their generation or status, just like the feudal order of importance or seniority in China's ancient religious communities and temples.

After the guests sit at the table, the host or hostess begins to operate in strict accordance with the old tea rules, particular about teasets, water quality, tea leaves, and the ways of making and drinking tea.

The teaset includes the teapot, teacups and the utensil for containing tea dregs. The teapot is tiny, just like a persimmon. The ceramic teacups have very thin walls. The ceramic utensil for containing tea dregs, like a drum, is composed of a plate, which looks like the surface of a drum, and a tube-shaped porcelainware. The plate has small holes, through which the tea to rince teacups at the beginning of the ceremony leaks. Boiling water poured on the lid of the teapot to keep the inside tea warm also leaks through the holes. The utensil for containing tea dregs also holds the remaining water and tea. The kong fu tea ceremony is particular about the teapot. After the Ming and Qing dynasties, teapots made from purple sand were specially used because of the idea that tea art should return to its original nature, but the teapot used in the Chaozhou and Shantou gong fu tea ceremony is made from the soft earth of Chaozhou, for this kind of teapot absorbs the fragrance of tea more easily. Talking of this, we should know that different teas need to be poured into different teapots. For example, scented tea needs porcelain teapots to keep its fragrance; it is better to use china teapots or glasses, rather than sand pots, to hold weak green tea so as to keep the fragrance of the tea and observe the shape and color of the tea leaves. Red tea (black tea) or semi-fermented (oolong) tea needs sand tea pots, which give an impression of primitive simplicity and can easily send forth the fragrance of the tea. Before a new teapot is formally used, it must first be soaked in first-made tea water for over three months to keep the teapot fragrant all over. Teapots made of Chaozhou earth contain a fragrance themselves. The teacups are exquisitely small like walnuts or almonds, but are simple and strong.

A Classified Collection of Writings on Various Subjects of the Qing Dynasty, a sketchbook written by Xu Ke, was classified into 92 subjects, such as seasons, geography, diplomacy, customs, craft and literature, and included more than 13,500 items. It collected hundreds of notes by writers of the Qing Dynasty, with newspapers as its reference material. The book tells an interesting story which demonstrates the importance of soaking the teapot with tea water before it is formally used. It was said that a rich man of Chaozhou liked tea very much. One day, a beggar came up to his door. Leaning against the door, the beggar begged for tea instead of food, saying, "I hear you have the nicest tea. Could you give me a pot of it?" The rich man felt it ridiculous to hear this. He said, "Could it be said that you, a beggar, have an idea of tea?" The beggar said, "I was once rich. But as I indulged in tea all day I became a beggar. Now I have to make a living by begging to support my family." Hearing this, the rich man readily gave him a cup of quality kong fu tea, for he thought that he had met a bosom tea friend. After tasting the tea, the beggar said, "Sure enough you made nice tea, but it is not mellow enough, for you used a new teapot." Then the beggar took out an old light-colored teapot out of his sleeves. When the pot lid was opened, fragrance struck the nose. The beggar said that though he was penniless and often suffered from cold and hunger, he took the teapot with him all the time. The rich man liked the teapot so much that he wanted to pay 3,000 taels of gold for it. But the beggar hated to part with it. He said, "I want only half of the money you offered, but could we two share the teapot?" The rich man gladly accepted it. From then on they became close friends. This story tells us that it takes a lot of time to soak the teapot with tea water before tea is made.

Making tea needs superior skills.

After the guest is seated, the host puts Tie Guanyin, a variety of oolong tea, into a small teapot. The tea leaves may account for 70 percent of the volume of the teapot, so that they extend to the top of the teapot after soaking. The tea made the first time is used for washing cups rather than drinking, creating an artistic atmosphere of tea in every sense. Then the host pours boiling water into the teapot. This time the tea leaves are exposed and send forth their fragrance. The host begins to offer tea to the guests. He places four small cups in a circle, and then shuttles among them with the small teapot in his hand until each cup is filled 70 percent of its volume with tea. At this time the tea made for the second time is precisely used up. This way of serving tea is called "Lord Guan Patrolling the City." The rest of the tea is poured into the four cups little by little, which is called "Marquis Han Xin Gathering His Troops." The four cups put together implies the gathering of host and guests. "Lord Guan Patrolling the City" shows not only superior skills but also complete success according to Chinese philosophy, and "Marquis Han Xin Gathering His Troops" indicates the great harmony reflected in the sharing of the essence of tea. In the pouring, the host's expertise is demonstrated if the tea in the four small cups have the same color in different layers. If the tea has different colors each time the host adds boiling water, he is really a master tea-maker.

The host then holds the small cups of tea before the guests. He first serves the chief guest, and then the other guests according to their generation and age. Finally the host himself joins them. There are special skills of tasting this kind of tea. Instead of drinking the tea in one mouthful, you should let it turn around your tongue and fully realize its fragrance before you swallow it. Then you must show the bottom of the teacup to the host to express your sincere gratitude as well as your praise for his superior skills.

After several rounds of drinking, which display the friendship between the host and the guests as well as the pleasure of tasting tea, the tea has sent forth nearly all its fragrance. In the last round of drinking, the host takes the tea leaves out of the teapot with a bamboo clip and puts them in a tiny cup to let the guests enjoy the beautiful natural tea leaves and at the same time to show them that he will not make tea with these used tea leaves again. This kind of kong fu tea is not made only by the rich. Small workshops and stalls in Chaozhou and Shantou sell it by the roadside. Even farmers there who carry produce down the mountains pull out teasets, heat up water and make tea in the mountains when they take a rest. And it is routine for them to make this kind of tea when they are at home resting. At hotels and restaurants in modern cities and towns, kong fu tea is also made at counters to receive guests. People present the tea as gifts to those whom they ask for help, or sell the tea in small bags, each of which contains the amount used in one teapot. It can be seen from this that kong fu tea is well popularized in Chaozhou and Shantou as a genuine folk art. In addition, kong fu tea demands particular water requirements. Mountain farmers are not very rich, but still quite a few old people of Chaozhou and Shantou buy mountain spring water to make tea. People of Chaozhou and Shantou are tightly bound to the simple teasets, which create profound friendship. Once drinking this kind of tea, farmers toiling at work all day will feel as if fragrance has arisen from below their tongues, and feel no longer tired.

The Chaozhou and Shantou kong fu tea is rich in connotations.

It has the courtesy advocated by the Confucian spirit, beautiful teasets and brilliant tea culture, the complete unity of the spiritual and the material as well as of form and content, the philosophy of the co-existence of smallness and bigness, cleverness and clumsiness, falseness and truth, and waxing and waning, the Chinese people's pursuit of a happy and rich life and spirit of sharing joys and sorrows. Who dare say that the Chinese tea culture no longer prospers?

The Yunnan Tea Ceremony

China is the homeland of tea, and the Yunnan-Guizhou Plateau is the place where Chinese tea originated. Since Yunnan Province has both the human environment and the natural environment fit for planting tea, it is said to have "the best camellia in the world." The nine-procedure tea and the three-taste tea are representative of the Yunnan tea culture.

The nine-procedure tea is used by scholarly families of Kunming to entertain guests. Scholars of Kunming, which is known as the flower city, love flowers. Generally speaking, the host plants various rare flowers at home and hangs some tea-related paintings on the wall, which serve as a foil for tea drinking.

Since Lu Yu wrote *The Book of Tea,* the Chinese people have advocated telling stories about tea and enjoying the sight of tea paintings as they drink tea. The nine-procedure tea means the nine procedures of tea art, i.e., appraising tea, washing teasets, putting tea leaves into the teapot, pouring hot water into the teapot, stirring the tea, pouring the tea into teacups, offering tea to the guests, and drinking tea together. These jobs are often done by the Yunnan girls, who are beautiful and graceful by nature. They may take their parents' hint, and set out some rare teas for the guests to appraise and choose. This choice is determined by the natural conditions of Yunnan Province, for in other parts of China, it is not easy to get even one kind of fine tea, to say nothing of selecting one kind from many. After the guests finish selecting one kind of tea leaves, the girl washes clean the wax-printed tea cloth and all sorts of teasets before the guests, puts tea leaves into the teapot, pours hot water into it, and then stirs the tea. When the sweet smell of the tea floats in the air and the color of the tea is just right, the girl pours the tea into the teacups adeptly and gracefully, and presents the cups one after another to the guests according to the order of their age, generation, or status. When the host says "Have a cup of tea, please," the guests may drink the tea. After several rounds of drinks, the host will tell some stories or legends about tea, and talk about the beautiful scenery of Yunnan Province. The beauty of the home province of tea, as well as the friendship of the host, is reflected through the nine-procedure tea.

The three-taste tea of the Bais has another kind of flavor. The tea is generally made by girls, too. The first bowl for you is sugared tea, which wishes you happiness. The second is bitter tea with no condiments. At this time the host and the guests can chat about domestic trivialities, hard times of the past, or some moving stories about a hard but happy life. Take this story for example. Once there was a beautiful kingdom, where the tyrant ate people's eyes and destroyed everything beautiful. Then a brave young man asked for help from a wild cat, who bit the throat of the tyrant and brought happy life to people again. Bitter tea can help you to distinguish the true, the good and the beautiful from the false, the evil and the disgraceful, and remind you of the joys and sorrows of life. The last bowl is the chewable rice flower tea, which wishes you good luck. These ways of life are contained in the three-taste tea of the Bais.

Chapter 9
Tea Customs of Ethnic
Groups of China

Tea Customs in Yunnan, Guizhou
and Sichuan Provinces

The ethnic groups of Southwest China live in concentrated communities in Yunnan, Guizhou and Sichuan provinces. As original tea-growing areas, these places are rich in tea culture. In particular, when the traditional tea culture fell into decay in modern times in the Central Plains (comprising the middle and lower reaches of the Yellow River), many tea ceremonies and customs survived in the southwest because the simple folkways and the local culture were less affected by foreign culture.

According to historical information, ethnic groups of Southwest China knew, used and planted tea earlier than those of the Central Plains.

This can be proved by the story about Yao Bai, who planted tea and distributed land among the Jinuos of Yunnan Province. Long, long ago, there lived an ancestress of the Jinuos, whose name was Yao Bai. She not only created heaven and earth, but also decided to distribute land to the ethnic groups. The Jinuos, however, failed to attend the meeting at which the land was distributed, for they did not like the probable disputes during the distribution. Angry as she was, Yao Bai was afraid that they would be badly off later without land. So she scattered a handful of seeds down from a mountain top. From that time, tea trees grew in the Longpa Village, where the Jinuos started to plant and use tea. The high mountain where they lived became one of the six tea mountains of Yunnan Province. The story about Yao Bai's planting tea brought a history of tea planting to the first stage of human civilization.

The ethnic groups of Southwest China used and produced tea earlier than people of the Central Plains. Most tea historians hold that people successively used tea as herbs, food and drink. The Jinuos have regarded tea as a "cold dish in sauce" to the present day. When you come to their villages, they will collect fresh tea leaves at once, crumple and knead them into soft and thin pieces, put them in a large bowl, and add some yellow fruit juice, sour bamboo shoots, sour ants, garlics, chili and salt. Then they will ask you to taste their special "cold dishes in sauce."

Some ethnic groups, such as the Yi, Bai, Wa and Lahu, have the habit of drinking "roast tea." The tea is roasted in pots or bamboo tubes, or on steel plates. For example, the Lahus roast tea by shaking an earthenware pot on a burning stove. When the tea turns brown, they pour boiling water into the pot. The tea roasted in this way gives off rich fragrant smells. The Wa nationality roast tea on the thin steel plate, and then put the roasted tea into a pot and pour in boiling water. The Bais have a way of roasting tea similar to that of the Lahus except that they add condiments such as sugar and rice flowers to the tea. They also endow the tea with cultural meaning such as sweetness first, bitterness second, and recollections last.

The bamboo tube tea, which is popular among some ethnic groups in Yunnan Province, is also noteworthy. Perhaps this tea is a transition from loose tea to lump tea by pressing while roasting them. The bamboo tube tea of the Dais is an example. When you climb into a bamboo building of the Dais, a girl in a tight skirt and with a silver belt greets you at once, and the oldest man treats you to the bamboo tube tea. The girl puts tea leaves into a new, fragrant bamboo tube, and the elderly man places it onto a tripod on the stove to soften, evaporate and roast the tea indirectly instead of scorching it. In about six to seven minutes, the tea-maker will press the tea leaves in the bamboo tube with a stick, stuff raw tea leaves, and continue to roast until the bamboo tube is filled with tea leaves. After the tea leaves get dry, the tube is cut open and the cylinder-shaped bamboo tube tea leaves are ready. By breaking off some dry tea leaves, putting them into a bowl, and pouring some boiling water, the host can treat you to a bowl of tea with the fragrance of both bamboo and roasted tea leaves. From the process of producing roasted tea, we can see the customs of roasting tea left over by the Tang Dynasty (618-907), and the original form of "lump tea processed by pressing" as well. The round tea cake, popular in the Yangtze River in the Tang Dynasty, perhaps evolved from the roast tea of boundary ethnic groups, who processed tea with the natural and primitive tools of bamboo tubes, while people in the Central Plains processed tea by pressing with molds.

From the above-mentioned examples, we can see the original forms of processing tea either by roasting and pressing and the use of it as a vegetable. Tea arose in the Yunnan-Guizhou Plateau, entered Sichuan Province along the Yangtze River, and then reached Hunan and Hubei provinces through the Three Gorges. People in tea's original growing area must have had a special method of processing it. The sour-ant cold tea in sauce made by the boundary people was followed by tea used by people in the Central Plains as vegetables; tea roasted by the boundary people in pots or bamboo tubes or on steel plates was followed by tea roasted by Lu Yu and tea roasted after evaporation; the cylinder-shaped tea roasted and pressed in bamboo tubes was followed by the perforated tea of the Tang Dynasty, the cake-shaped tea of the Song (420-479) and Yuan (1271-1368) dynasties, and the present-day brick-shaped tea and bowl-shaped tea.

Tibetan Tea Culture

Princess Wencheng and the History of Tibetans' Tea Drinking

The Tibetans started to drink tea early in the mid-700s in the Tang Dynasty. This reminds us of Princess Wencheng, the envoy of the friendship between the Hans and the Tibetans. In A.D. 633, Tibetan King Songzan Gambo put down the rebellion in northern Tibet. To strengthen contact with the Central Plains, he sent an envoy to Chang'an (today's Xi'an, Shaanxi Province) to request unity by marriage in the 15th year of Zhenguan (A.D. 641) of the Tang Dynasty. The Tang emperor Taizong decided to marry his daughter, Princess Wencheng, to Songzan Gambo. When she went to Tibet, Princess Wencheng took many craftsmen and materials, which were said to include 3,800 kind of seeds, as well as skills of metallurgy, spinning and weaving, silk reeling, papermaking and winemaking. Besides, she introduced the custom of drinking tea to Tibet. In the Tang Dynasty, when tea culture came into being in the Central Plains, many people went to Tibet with methods of tea drinking and tea ceremonies and culture. *Jia,* the name used for tea in the Tang Dynasty in some parts of China, has been used in Tibetan to the present, which shows that the Tibetans started to drink tea early in the Tang Dynasty. In the *Supplement to the History of the Tang* by a Tang writer are the words: "Once Duke Changlu was sent to Tibet as an envoy. When he was making tea in his tent, the Tibetan king asked him what he was making. Duke

Changlu said, 'It is tea, which can remove worry as well as thirst.' The king said that he also had tea. Then Duke Changlu asked him to show his tea. The king put out his tea of various kinds, and pointed at the tea with his fingers, saying, 'This is Shouzhou tea, this is Shuzhou tea, this is Guzhu tea, this is Qimen tea, and this is Changming tea.'" This shows that the royal Tibetan court knew a lot about the tea of the Central Plains during the 200 years after Princess Wencheng went to Tibet. South of the Tibetan mountain areas, a popular folk song titled the *Princess Brings the Dragon-Design Tea Cup,* says, "The dragon-design teacup was brought into Tibet by Princess Wencheng. It reminds us of her kindly face." This shows that Princess Wencheng brought to Tibet not only tea leaves, but also teasets. The tea cakes, popular in the Tang Dynasty, were further changed into those with the delicate design of dragon or phoenix, which were, according to the Tibetans, brought to Tibet by Princess Wencheng. The Tibetans also think that Princess Wencheng taught them how to grind and boil tea. Whenever they treat their guests to tea, they will tell how Princess Wencheng taught the ancient Tibetan women to make milky tea and buttered tea. Princess Wencheng did introduce tea culture to Tibet, even if these folk songs or legends about her are exaggerated.

Afterwards, during the former Shu and the latter Shu of the Five Dynasties and the Song Dynasty, people exchanged horses for tea with the Tibetans, bringing the custom of drinking tea of the Central Plains to Tibet. Most Tibetans, who led a nomadic life, ate cheese rather than vegetables, and tea helped them digest the cheese. On the dry plateau, drinking tea, which helped them not only produce saliva and quench thirst but also prevented many local common diseases, was popular with officials and the common people. Therefore, Tibetans regard tea as something holy rather than something common. According to them, "One will get dull without tea in a day, and sick without tea in three days."

Tea Culture in Tibetan Temples

In the development of tea culture of the Central Plains, Buddhism played an important role. The Tibetans, who believe in Buddhism, attach importance to tea ceremonies during Buddhist activities. They often connect tea with God. When praying to deities in temples, they take medicine, holy water, and tea with them. In the Zuglakhang Monastery in Lhasa, brick tea over one hundred years old was collected, which, though actually useless, was treated by the monks as treasures to protect the Temple. Therefore, the Tibetans think of tea as something more holy than the Hans do. Regarded as something pure and holy granted by Buddha, tea requires very solemn ceremony. More than 200 years ago, a Portuguese missionary wrote *My Travels from Tartary to Tibet, China,* in which he gave a detailed description of the tea culture in Tibetan temples. He wrote, "The Tibetans have a surprising way of drinking tea. The tea bricks were of high quality, and five such tea bricks were valued at one tael of silver. All the teapots were made of silver. The teapots and teacups on golden saucers on the sacrificial altar in the Lama temple, which were all made of emerald, looked gorgeous. In particular, the Kewenbamu Lamasery, which was the religious and cultural center, was the most magnificent. Many scholars and pilgrims from all parts of China gathered here to have a tea party. The devout pilgrims treated the Lamaists to tea. It took a lot of money to hold such a simple but momentous activity. Each of the 4,000 Lamaists drank two cups of tea, which cost 56 taels of silver. The ceremony of presenting tea to Lamaists was also a surprise. Some young men held steaming hot boiler for the benefactors kneeling on the ground to give to the countless rows of Lamaists in solemn robes, who sat still. At this time the benefactors would sing hymns. Rich pilgrims would serve tea with refreshments or cheese at the tea party."

The above-mentioned materials show at least the following points:

1. Tea is vested with mystery in Tibetan temples. It has more spiritual meaning than material meaning. The Buddhists and Taoists on the Central Plains drink tea mainly to cultivate their moral character by sitting in meditation and to avoid dozing off, though they connect tea drinking with Buddhist or Taoist activities, while in Tibetan temples, tea is regarded as a holy and pure thing similar to charms, holy water and treasures.

2. The Tibetan temples are particular about tea art. Their teasets, for example, are not inferior to those of rich Han families, though they are no match for the royal court of the Central Plains. The tea, contained in boiler, is drunk in combination with the charity of the temples, as Tibetan tea culture not only absorbs the idea of charity in the tea culture of the Central Plains, but also contains Buddhism.

3. The tea ceremonies of Tibetan temples, grand, solemn and large in scale, is different from those of the Tang Dynasty monks in the Central Plains, who decocted and boiled tea anywhere. The large-scale tea party perhaps, was, either influenced by the large-scale tea parties of temples in the Song Dynasty, or created by the Tibetans. At the tea parties, the Tibetans give Buhhdist salutes and sing paeans under the command of the abbot. Unlike the monks of the Central Plains, who drink tea to achieve peace of mind and find their true selves, the Buddhists of the Tibetan temples treat the tea they drink as something holy and miraculous bestowed on them by the spirits of the nirvana. This clearly shows their objective idealism, greatly different to reformed Chinese Buddhism, is more similar to the original form of Buhhdism.

Treating Guests to Buttered Tea and Milky Tea, and the Tibetan Festivals and Customs

Unlike some upper-class Tibetans, who drink Maojian tea or

Yaxi tea, the common Tibetans or Lamaists mainly drink Kangzhuan tea, Fuzhuan tea, Jinjian tea and Fangbao tea. Buttered tea and green tea are drunk in both pastoral areas and agricultural areas. In pastoral areas milky tea is also popular.

Milky tea is the Tibetans' main drink with rice or bread. The Tibetans generally drink several bowls of milky tea in the morning before going to work. They drink it five or six times from morning till night. Milky tea is not only for daily use, but also for the reception of guests. Whenever a distinguished guest comes, they make mellow milky tea. First, they pound brick tea into pieces, and put them into the teapot to boil. Then they pour the hot, fragrant tea into a wooden vat over one meter high, put in some butter and salt, and mix with a stick. At this time, the tea, water, butter and salt are dissolved. Then heating the tea in the teapot again, they finally get fragrant buttered tea. When a distinguished guest comes, they often present *hada* (a piece of white silk used as a greeting gift among the Tibetans) to him, let him take a seat, and then offer him buttered tea. The Tibetans stress etiquette when drinking milky tea. The host must continually add milky tea to the guest's bowl after he drinks, while the guest must, instead of drinking up the bowl of tea at one gulp, leave half bowl of the tea for the host to add more. If the host fills up the guest's bowl, the guest, who cannot drink any more, may not drink again. But at the time for leave, he must drink up the bowl at one gulp to express his thanks and satisfaction to the host.

Tibetan herdsmen are very hospitable. When a close friend or a new guest comes into one of their tents, the hostess, after bowing, immediately serves milky tea. Then the hostess puts ginseng, rice, steamed stuffed buns and other food on a plate, which is covered with *hada* to show respect for the guest. The most honored guest can seize meat and stewed vegetables to eat with his hands.

For Tibetans, tea implies friendship, respect, purity and

auspiciousness. During their festivals, they drink buttered tea and barley wine while singing and dancing merrily. In the Taer Temple, Qinghai Province, there is a lantern show, with buttered tea as the theme.

In the Zhongdian region of the northwest part of Yunnan Province, people hold a special tea party with antiphons. In slack seasons, young people stay in the fields and on the roads. Boys and girls respectively select one of them as a representative, and the boy and the girl selected, on the pretext of grabbing a scarf or a cap, chase each other and leave the crowd to discuss when and where to hold such a tea party. When the guests arrive, the host or the hostess sings loudly, "Honored guests, we have the nerve to invite you into our humble village to drink tea with us. Your promise will be our privilege." At this time the guests invited politely sing, "Oh, honored people, we don't deserve to accept your invitation. Please invite other girls." This results in antiphons. With a bowl of tea followed by a song, the two sides sing to each other alternately until one side admits defeat.

Tibetans use tea in various polite formalities and customs, such as weddings, childbirth, funerals and religious rites. When a baby is born, they first boil tea, with the fresh tea implying good looks. At wedding parties, a lot of tea is boiled, the bright and fresh tea expressing a happy marriage. In funerals tea is also boiled, the light tea expressing people's mourning for the deceased. When visiting Lamaists, Tibetan women must apply sugar or milky tea, which is thought of as something beautiful and pure, to their faces, or they will be punished.

Milky Tea on Plateaus and Grasslands

After tea arose in Yunnan and Guizhou provinces, it gradually began to be used in other places. It was largely used in two ways. One way was that it was used as medicinal herbs, a practice which then evolved into a tea cultural system, in which tea was drunk without refreshments. For instance, various schools of tea culture in the Central Plains of China, such as the Taoist tea culture, the Buddhist tea culture, and the Confucian tea culture, which was the mainstay of the tea cultures, along with the people of Korea, Japan and other countries in Southeast Asia believing in Confucianism, drink tea without refreshments. The other way was that tea was used as food, whence evolved a tea cultural system, in which tea was drunk with refreshments. For example, people south of the Yangtze River drink tea to go with condiments, while people in the northwest part of China and in some countries in Western Europe drink buttered tea or milky tea to go with brown sugar. It is reasonable for some people to hold that the culture of the northwest grasslands can be called the "milky tea culture," a title which reflects the connection between the life style of the people of northwest China, who made a living by grazing and hunting and who fed on mutton and beef, and the mountain forest farming culture. In some sense, tea played an epoch-making role for herdsmen and hunters after it entered grasslands and pasturelands. It is often said that people make a living according to given circumstances. On high mountains and grasslands in the northwest part of China, a large quantity of cattle, sheep, camels and horses, are raised. The milk and meat provide people with much heat but few vitamins. So tea supplements the basic needs of the nomadic tribes, whose diet lacks vegetables. Therefore, the herdsmen from Qinghai-Tibet Plateau and the Xinjiang and the Inner Mongolia autonomous regions follow the tea cultural system, in which they drink tea with milk, and make milky tea the most precious thing for the people in the northwest of China.

In the Xinjiang Uygur Autonomous Region, each person

consumes one *jin* (500 grams) of brick tea annually on average, and in the pastoral areas as well as the farming areas and grasslands, each person consumes 5.4 *jin* of brick tea annually on average. The herdsmen eat tea leaves while they drink tea. Many ethnic groups in the Region cannot go without pancakes of wheat or cornflour, or milky tea when they have meals or receive guests. In celebration of the Id al-fitr and Corban Festival, people present tea to each other as gifts, which stand for loyal sentiment, sincere wishes and pure friendship. For the Huis, tea symbolizes purity apart from a daily necessity.

The Mongolian grasslands are full of a rich flavor of fragrant milky tea. In spite of their frequent removal on their felted carts to where grass is luxuriant, the Mongolians never forget to boil milky tea. I, the author, was lucky to enjoy the Mongolian milky tea in the west of the Mongolian Grasslands. It was a late summer. Most of the grassland had turned yellowish, and only in a few low-lying places at the foot of the mountain was there still some green grass. In the northeast part of Shangjing of the Liao Dynasty were the tombs of Shengzong and other emperors, and on the undulating hills south of the tombs were scattered the tents of Mongolian herdsmen, and of a small number of Han herdsmen, who were perhaps Chinese-featured Qidan descendants. Our investigation group entered four or five Mongolian yurts. These days, the herdsmen have permanent residences, where they put valuable articles so each tent is simply furnished. About one *chi* (one-third of a meter) above the ground in the north was a heatable earth bed, covered with felt and quilts. Along the inside walls of the tent were simple articles of daily use. At the center of the tent was a stove, on which was a big kettle full of milky tea. To make tea, they first pound brick tea to pieces, then pour in water and boil the tea, filter the dregs, add the appropriate amount of milk, continue to boil, and frequently ladle out some and pour it. The system is much like Lu

Yu's way of making tea. On arrival, we sat beside the host according to their status and generation, while their Mongolian guide sat in a right-hand seat. The women operated near the far end of the seats. First, the hostess put before us a small table on the felted mattress, and placed several bowls on the table. They contained millet stir-fried milky beancurd, salt and sugar. Then the hostess put several bowls of brown milky tea before us. The guests should not drink the tea up at one gulp, but allow the hostess to continually add tea to their bowls, in the same way as they drink buttered tea. The herdsmen generally add salt when they drink milky tea, but when treating guests to tea they add white sugar and salt to show their special respect for the guests. The stir-fried millet, called broom corn millet by the Mongolians, is hard to chew. The guide said that, according to the hostess, we could drink milky tea to go with the millet. Large cakes of milky beancurd, like exceptionally big cakes of soap, were hung out on the tents to dry. After eating only a small cake of it, you will not feel hungry for half a day. When they entertain guests, the herdsmen cut the milky beancurd into square pieces, and let the guests eat it with white sugar. If you only eat it occasionally, you will not be accustomed to its bitter taste, but the fragrance of milky tea can help remove the bitterness. After having had these foods, I further understood why the herdsmen think of tea as life. Milk, milky beancurd and stir-fried millet are indigestible, and vegetables are scarce on the grasslands, so tea is the unique food that can aid digestion and increase vitamins. The stir-fried millet is not often eaten, except for long journeys or the entertainment of guests. The milky beancurd, as a fine quality dairy product, is also precious. Therefore, milky tea becomes the Mongolians' main food. After blessing the hostess, the guests can drink up the last bowl of milky tea. Then, the guests make a bow to express their thanks, and the host and hostess go out of the tent and see them off, thus putting an end to the entertainment of guests with milky tea. When we walked out of the tent and seeing the blue sky, white clouds, cattle, sheep, and lush grass, we had gained a new understanding of the milky tea culture on the grasslands.

On the Mongolian grasslands, milky tea is used not only in daily life and the entertainment of guests, but also in grand festivals. For example, after the Mongolians ask Lamaists to chant scriptures, they present *hada* and several pieces of brick tea to the Lamaists. In autumn, at temple fairs or the Nadam Fair, people will entertain customers with milky tea, and brick tea is of course on sale on a large scale.

Likewise, other northwest ethnic groups also like to drink milky tea. As well, they use milky tea in weddings.

It is noteworthy that milky tea is also served to Buddha and gods because most northwest ethnic groups believe in Buddhism, which is irrevocably committed to tea. Confucians of the Central Plains examined themselves with tea and obtained spiritual strength from it, while northern ethnic groups serve tea to Buddha and gods and seek to free themselves from worldly worries. The spiritual sense of tea is stressed by all ethnic groups of China, a rare occurrence in world dietary history.

The Manchus' Contributions to Tea Culture

The Manchus in the Qing Dynasty were descendants of Nüzhen. The Nüzhens started to drink tea early in the Liao (916-1125) and Jin (1115-1234) dynasties. According to records of the Song Dynasty (960-1279), many customs of a matriarchal system were retained among the Nüzhens in the late Liao Dynasty and the early Jin Dynasty. At that time sweethearts could run away freely, and later visit and present gifts to the girl's family. When the son-in-law called on his wife's family, all females of the family, young or old, would sit on the heatable bed for him to make a bow to. Then his wife's family would warmly entertain him with tea, liquor, cheese and candied fruit, etc. The Nüzhens called food served on festivals and food served to guests "tea food," which showed the role that tea played in their life.

With the rise of the Manchus, it became a common practice for the northern ethnic groups to drink tea. And the descendants of the Nüzhens still liked to drink tea. After the reign of Emperor Qianlong, emperors were addicted to tea, making it popular with the Manchus. The Manchus made outstanding contributions to tea culture.

First, the Manchus organically connected the tea culture that was characterized by serving tea without refreshments and the tea culture characterized by serving tea with refreshments, and they put the milky tea culture to a position almost equal with that characterized by serving tea without refreshments. In the Qing Dynasty emperors and empresses liked to eat dairy products and drink milky tea. At the old men's banquet, which started at the time of Emperor Kangxi, the officials in charge of tea and meals first presented a cup of brown milky tea to the emperor and his sons, respectively. After the emperor and the crown prince drank the milky tea, the officials presented tea without refreshments to ministers. This shows the Manchu emperors had inherited the northern hobby of drinking milky tea. The introduction of milky tea to the imperial court affirmed the important position of the tea culture characterized by serving tea with refreshments. According to *Records from the Yangji House,* the Manchus "used to drink milky tea. Rules were made to provide cows for the emperor and his officials. Milk was sent to the tea house for boiling, and milky cakes were made in the tea house in spring and autumn." The herdsmen and hunters on grasslands liked to drink tea to go with milk, while the Nüzhens used to drink tea to go with such refreshments as tea cakes and tea medicine. It can be seen from this that the Manchus had three sources of tea culture: first, since the Liao and Jin dynasties they had adopted the northwest ethnic groups' custom of drinking milky tea; second, they followed the Nüzhens' custom of drinking tea to go with fruits and refreshments; third, they inherited the Hans' custom of drinking tea without refreshments. Emperor Qianlong drank milky tea both at court in his daily life and at old men's banquets; but when he was present at tea banquets or was composing poems or painting pictures, he became a bosom friend of Confucian tea drinkers, for he liked to drink tea without refreshments. Thus, the Manchus drew together the tea customs of ethnic groups of the Central Plains, the northwest and the northeast. Most orthodox Chinese tea-drinkers advocate Confucians' drinking tea without refreshments rather than drinking tea with refreshments or drinking milky tea. However, the tea culture characterized by drinking tea with refreshments plays a noticeable role not only in China but throughout the world. According to statistics, 1.3-1.5 billion people in the world drink tea without refreshments, with the annual sales of tea being 400,000-450,000 tons, while 100 million Chinese and 3.8-4.0 billion people from other countries drink tea with refreshments. At present, most typical tea houses in Beijing sell both tea and food, which is the result of the connection of drinking tea with refreshments and drinking tea without refreshments. Adding fragrance of flowers to tea conflicts with the traditional tea culture. We should notice that the tea culture characterized by drinking tea with refreshments is popular among people. So we can say that the Manchus made creative contributions to tea culture.

Second, as the imperial family of the Qing Dynasty liked to drink scented tea, semi-fermented tea (a sort of scented tea between black tea and green tea) developed rapidly. The jade perfume was favored by the common people, though it was looked down upon in traditional tea culture. Semi-fermented tea pushed forward the changing of Chinese tea culture. The "Eight Banners" (military-administrative organizations of the Manchus in the Qing Dynasty), an idle class, combined tea with flowers and created many kinds of tea, undoutedly enriching Chinese tea culture.

Third, teacups with lids were popular with the imperial family of the Qing Dynasty. As the Manchus lived in a cold zone in the north, it was necessary for them to keep the tea in the teacups warm with lids. A pioneering work of teasets, the lids keep the tea warm and clean, dispel tea leaves, and cover the mouth to show respect for others.

The common people of the Manchus often treated guests to tea at home. In all, the Manchus played an important role in the combination of the tea cultures of all ethnic groups, as well as in the development of tea art and tea ceremonies.

Chapter 10
Chinese Tea Culture Spreads Worldwide

The Spread of Chinese Tea Culture to Japan and Korea

The spread of Chinese tea and tea culture to eastern countries, especially to Japan and Korea, is noticeable. There are several reasons for the spread. Civilized early, Korea and Japan, like China, have many detailed records about the spread of tea and culture. According to historical documents and cultural relics excavated, China is the cultural source of Korea and Japan. Therefore, Korea and Japan absorbed not only Chinese tea, but also its material and spiritual forms. Korea and Japan, where tea is drunk without refreshments, imported Chinese tea just after the Saint of Tea Lu Yu established the system of tea culture in the Tang Dynasty. Every change of the tea culture from the Tang Dynasty to the Ming Dynasty spread abroad, and Korean and Japanese students studying in China were first enlightened by the Chinese culture.

According to records, in 593, in the reign of Emperor Wendi of the Sui Dynasty (581-601), China introduced tea to Japan along with the spread of its culture, art and Buddhism to apan. During the reign of Emperor Xuanzong of the Tang Dynasty, on April 8, 729, which was the first year of the reign of Mikado Amahira, a grand tea drinking activity was held in the Japanese royal court. That day, Mikado gathered 100 monks to expound the texts of Buddhism in the royal residence. The next day, the monks were granted tea. Over 70 years later, the founder of the Japanese Tiantai (Tien-tai) Sect of Buddhism, came to China in 804 (the 20th year of Zhenyuan during the reign of Emperor Dezong of the Tang Dynasty). The next year (the first year of Yongzhen during the reign of Emperor Shunzong of the Tang Dynasty), he returned to his country with a lot of Buddhist scriptures and Chinese tea seeds, which were planted on a Mountain near a river. Another outstanding Japanese monk came to China also in 804, but returned to Japan in 806. He learned the Truth-Word Sect of Buddhism in Chang'an (today's Xi'an), China. When he returned to Japan, he took with him tea seeds, a stone mortar with which to process tea, as well as the skills of processing tea by steaming, pounding and roasting. At that time, encouraged by the monks, the Japanese started to drink tea as people of the Tang Dynasty did. They boiled cake tea, and added such condiments as sweet kudzu vines and ginger. Owing to the limited quantity of tea trees planted, only the royal family and a small number of monks drank tea at the time.

After the reign of Hirayasu, Japan made fewer contacts with China over almost 200 years from the Five Dynasties (907-960) to the Song and Liao dynasties. For some reasons, tea was stamped out in Japan. It was not until the Southern Song Dynasty (1127- 1279) that Japanese monk Eisai reintroduced tea into Japan.

When he was 14 years old, Eisai left home and was initiated into monkhood, studying in the Buddhist institute of the highest learning dedicated to the Japanese Tiantai sect. At the age of 21, he was determined to study in China. In the fourth year (1168) of Qiandao during the reign of Emperor Xiaozong of the Southern Song Dynasty, Eisai started off in Mingzhou Prefecture, Zhejiang Province, traveled through famous mountains and visited magnificent temples south of the Yangtze River, paid respects to Master Xu'an of the Chan Sect at the Longevity Temple on the Tiantai Mountain, and moved to the Jingde Temple on the Tongshan Mountain with Master Xu'an. At that time tea drinking prevailed, and Eisai enjoyed the local customs. He lived in China for 24 years, and returned to Japan in the third year (1192) of Shaoxi during the reign of Guangzong of the Song Dynasty. Therefore, Eisai knew not only the general skills of Chinese tea art, but also the tea art of the Chan Sect. This is one of the major reasons why the Japanese tea art specially stresses Dhyana. After he returned to Japan, Eisai personally planted tea trees, and wrote *Health Preserving by Drinking Tea,* which absorbed the ideas of *The Book of Tea* by Lu Yu, and specially stressed such functions of tea as health care and cultivation of one's moral character. Eisai was the real founder of the Japanese tea art.

In the Yuan (1271-1368) and Ming (1368-1644) dynasties, Japanese monks continued to come to China. In particular, eminent Japanese monks mastered the tea-drinking skills of both the Ming Buddhist monks and the scholars, combined their skills, and created the Japanese tea art, which started to reach perfection. It can be seen from the above that the Japanese introduced, and then, according to their own national traits, improved Chinese tea art and the skills of planting, producing and drinking tea. It is not, therefore, a surprise that the Japanese retained the ancient Chinese tea art and formed a branch of the Chinese tea culture.

According to reliable records, tea was introduced from China into Korea during the period from 632 to 646. From then on, the Chinese custom of drinking tea and Chinese tea art were introduced into Korea. On the tablet inscription for Master Zhenjian, an eminent Korean monk (755-850) who set up the Double Stream Temple in Korea, was written, "If the Chinese tea is received again, put it into a stone pot and boil it with firewood."

Drinking tea became a ceremony in Korean temples during this period. The book *Travels in the South* by a Korean writer, who mastered the skills of making tea, reads "I had intended to boil tea to present the revered Xiao, but found no spring water. Suddenly the spring water in the rock crack gushed out, smelling sweet like milk. So I tried making tea with the spring water." It can be seen from this that Korean monks not only boiled tea in ceremonies, but also paid attention to tea art and the quality of water used to make tea. In 828 (the second year of Dahe during the reign of Emperor Wenzong of the Tang Dynasty), an envoy from Korea took tea seeds away with him from China.

From then on, the Koreans started to plant and produce tea. At present, Koreans produce more than 1.5 million kilograms of tea annually in over 20,000 mu (1,334 hactares) of major tea plantations.

It is generally thought that Chinese tea was introduced into South Asia in the Northern (960-1127) and Southern (1127-1279) Song dynasties. The Northern Song government established maritime tax supervisorates in Guangzhou, Mingzhou, Hangzhou and Quanzhou. Tea was exported to Southeast Asia through Guangzhou, Quanzhou, and to Japan and Korea through Mingzhou.

In the Southern Song Dynasty, the Chinese did business with Arabia, Palestine, Italy, Japan, India and other countries. Foreign businessmen often traveled between ports of China. At that time, Quanzhou, a major port opening to foreign countries, had frequent trade contacts with several Asian and African countries. Tea produced in Fujian Province was sold abroad in large quantities. In particular, Fengming Tea (today's Shiting Green Tea) produced in the Lotus Peak of Nan'an became a major product exported to South Asia, due to the fact that the tea helps digestion, diminishes inflammation, and increases the discharge of urine.

In the Ming Dynasty, Zheng He made voyages to the Western world seven times, and traveled through Viet Nam, Java, India, Sri

Lanka, the Arabian Peninsula and the eastern part of Africa, each time taking tea with him. At that time, tea drinking was popular in Southeast Asia.

The countries of Southeast Asia not only imported Chinese tea, but also introduced from China the skills for planting tea. Tea planting began in Indonesia in the 16th century, with the major plantations in Sumatra. In 1684 and 1731, Chinese tea seeds were introduced into Southeast Asia in large quantities. The year 1731, in particular, witnessed a remarkable success in the germination rate.

Tea was introduced to India by Tibetans. It is estimated that Indians started to get some idea of the skills of drinking Chinese tea in the Tang and Song dynasties. In 1780 and 1788 the East India Company imported some tea powder into India, which gradually became one of the big tea-producing countries.

It was of great importance that the countries of South Asia planted Chinese tea and formed the habit of drinking tea. This is because Chinese tea was exported by sea through these countries to the Mediterranean and European and African countries, and a tea route leading to the West developed after the Yuan and Ming dynasties. Through the countries of South Asia the Western countries imported the skills of planting and producing Chinese tea, produced large quantities of tea by virtue of the favorable natural conditions and the cheap labor force of Southeast Asia, and then transported the tea to Europe. This was much more convenient than the purchase of tea directly from China in the Ming Dynasty and the early Qing Dynasty. Therefore, the popularity of planting and drinking tea in South Asia not only reflected the extension of Chinese tea culture, but was also a prelude to the development and spread of Chinese tea culture towards the West. So further study of the custom of drinking tea in South Asia and its influence upon the West is a major requirement.

The Spread of Chinese Tea to the West

The spread of Chinese tea to the West largely underwent three periods.

The first period was during the Yuan Dynasty, when the West was forced to accept tea.

In the early part of the Yuan Dynasty, Genghis Khan and Hubilie mounted a large scale expedition. Since Mongolia was very early the transport station for the tea of the Central Plains to spread to the Central and West Asia, the Mongols cannot have gone without taking milky tea with them far to Europe via West Asia on this expedition. Eastern Europe probably got information about Chinese tea in this period, and it is likely that the expedition was connected to the fact that Russians imported tea from China later.

Naturally, there were some who gained information about Chinese tea on their own initiative. Chinese tea was seen in Western records in the Yuan Dynasty. Marco Polo, a famous Italian envoy as well as a friend of the Chinese people, came to China with his uncle from the north, traveling through Central Asia, Xingjiang, the northwest grasslands, Shangdu and Dadu. He stayed in China for more than ten years, and served as an official. At that time, people kept tea cakes, which had been used since the Tang and Song dynasties, as well as loose tea and the skill of stirring tea. Marco Polo, who maintained frequent contacts with the Chinese people, cannot have been unaware of their custom of drinking tea. Over ten years later, he returned to his country as an envoy of the Yuan government. This time he made his way from the south, traveling through the tea towns south of the Yangtze River, the countries of South Asia, the Indian Ocean and the Mediterranean. It is unknown whether he presented tea as gifts to the countries he traveled. However, according to the *Travels of Marco Polo*, which he wrote after he returned to his country, he took from China porcelain, macaroni and tea. The book was a sensation in the West, and Chinese tea has become a desired item among Europeans since then.

The second period was the Ming Dynasty, about the 16th century, when Chinese tea was exported on a small scale and was gradually spread abroad.

Russians got Chinese tea first. In 1567, when Emperor Muzong of the Ming Dynasty ascended the throne, two men from southern imperial Russia were said to have got Chinese tea and introduced it into Russia. In 1618, the Chinese ambassador in Russia presented a small amount of tea to the tsar. In 1735, the private trade caravans established during the reign of Empress Elizabeth traveled between China and Russia, and specially conveyed tea for the royal family, nobles and officials. Owing to the arduous transportation, the tea was expensive.

After the travels of Marco Polo, the European documents during the reign of Emperor Jiajing of the Ming Dynasty officially recorded tea drinking in China. At that time Lamaswar, a famous Venetian writer, wrote about his voyage and tea. Another book was titled *Chinese Tea*. From this period, the knowledge about tea drinking spread fully to Europe. Later, a Portuguese Catholic, wrote about Chinese tea in Portuguese after he returned to his country from China.

The third period was the period when Chinese tea was exported on a large scale and the tea trade gradually expanded.

The first period, accompanied by the rise of capitalism and the adoption of the colonial policy, was really created by the East India Company, which was set up in Holland in 1606. In 1607, Dutch ships reached Java, a Dutch colony. They arrived later in Macao, China, to carry green tea, and then returned to Europe in 1610. This was the beginning of Westners transporting tea from their colonies in the east, and the start of the importation of tea from China to

Western Europe. In 1637, ships of the British East India Company transported tea from Guangzhou, China. At the same time, the tea business between China and Britain started. Sweden, Holland, Denmark, France, Spain, Portugal, Germany, Hungary and some other countries later transported a huge amount of tea from China each year.

When tea was first taken to Europe, people did not know it very well. Many people still took a skeptical attitude towards tea until the 18th century when coffee began to be introduced into Europe; people had different views on the two new drinks. Tradition says that to get to the bottom of the matter, the Swedish King managed to find twin convicts sentenced to death to test whether tea and coffee did harm to people's health. The king said that if they agreed to test, they could be pardoned. Considering that they were likely to survive after the test, the twins agreed. Thus, every day one of them had several coffees, and the other drank several cups of tea. The test achieved an unprecedented success. The twin brothers lived many years without any trouble, and the twin who drank tea died at the age of 83. In this way, Chinese tea was finally accepted throughout Europe.

图书在版编目（CIP）数据

中国茶文化：英文/王玲著.
－北京：外文出版社，1999
ISBN 7-119-02144-3
I. 中… II. 王… III.茶叶－文化－专题研究—中国—英文
IV. G122

中国版本图书馆 CIP 数据核字（1999）第 03605 号

责任编辑　　白雪梅
封面设计　　唐少文

外文出版社网址：
　http://www.flp.com.cn
外文出版社电子信箱：
　info@flp.com.cn
　sales@flp.com.cn

中国茶文化

王玲　著

*

©外文出版社
外文出版社出版
（中国北京百万庄大街 24 号）
邮政编码　100037
北京外文印刷厂印刷
中国国际图书贸易总公司发行
（中国北京车公庄西路 35 号）
北京邮政信箱第 399 号　邮政编码　100044
2000 年(大 32 开)第 1 版
2001 年第 1 版第 2 次印刷
（英）
ISBN 7-119-02144-3/G・155(外)
02500(平)
7-E-3255 P